Retraining Your Brain with Cognitive Behavioral Therapy

The Basics and Beyond Workbook to Eliminate Anxiety, Depression, Anger, and Intrusive Thoughts In 7 Weeks with Over 10 Simple Strategies

George C. Dale

© **Copyright 2019 - All rights reserved.**

The content contained within this book may not be reproduced, duplicated or transmitted without direct written permission from the author or the publisher.

Under no circumstances will any blame or legal responsibility be held against the publisher, or author, for any damages, reparation, or monetary loss due to the information contained within this book. Either directly or indirectly.

Legal Notice
This book is copyright protected. This book is only for personal use. You cannot amend, distribute, sell, use, quote or paraphrase any part, or the content within this book, without the consent of the author or publisher.

Disclaimer Notice
Please note the information contained within this document is for educational and entertainment purposes only. All effort has been executed to present accurate, up to date, and reliable, complete information. No warranties of any kind are declared or implied. Readers acknowledge that the author is not engaging in the rendering of legal, financial, medical or professional advice. The content within this book has been derived from various sources. Please consult a licensed professional before attempting any techniques outlined in this book.

By reading this document, the reader agrees that under no circumstances is the author responsible for any losses, direct or indirect, which are incurred as a result of the use of information contained within this document, including, but not limited to, — errors, omissions, or inaccuracies.

Contents

Introduction _____ 1

Chapter 1:
Understanding the Basics of CBT _____ 5

Chapter 2:
Establish Your Goals _____ 20

Chapter 3:
Understanding Cognitive Distortion _____ 28

Chapter 4:
Break the Cycle of Negative Thoughts _____ 40

Chapter 5:
Understanding Depression _____ 51

Chapter 6:
CBT the Unique Depression Cure _____ 64

Chapter 7:
The Anxiety, Fear, Worry, Phobia Triggers _____ 75

Chapter 8:
Daily CBT Exercise for Anxiety, Fear, Worry, Phobia _____ 87

Chapter 9:
Identify what Unleashes the Hulk _____ 98

Chapter 10:
Anger Management CBT Techniques That Work_____ 109

Chapter 11:
Be Kind to Yourself with Self-Compassion_____ 119

Chapter 12:
Mindfulness Can Be the Difference Maker _____ 131

Conclusion _____ 144

Introduction

The rate at which the mental health of many people is spiraling downward is alarming. The state of mental health of a person is critical, as it affects how we function in life and with people around us. The pressures of work, family, and life in general have eaten so deep into many that it has taken its toll on mental health.

This calls for a quick intervention to get the mental health of people in check. A proven way to make this possible is through Cognitive Behavioral Therapy. Through the years, cognitive behavioral therapy has proven effective in helping people get a hold of their mental health. It has helped treat depression, various forms of anxiety disorders, phobias, sleep disorders, you name it.

It is a therapy which takes place in the form of a discussion between the client and the therapist. The therapist seeks to provide a solution to the client's problem through various kind of talking interaction.

Now, here is the problem.

George C. Dale

Not many people are comfortable sharing their feelings and private life with a stranger. Many people hate the openness and vulnerability it gives them. Besides, some people do not have access to a therapist. Others cannot afford the fees that come with going to a therapist.

Therefore, this manual aims to teach you how to be your own therapist. Relax, it is not as difficult as it sounds. Inscribed in the pages of this manual are proven techniques used by Cognitive Behavioral Therapists to help patients. This manual will hold you by the hand and guide you through the essential principles to help yourself.

Hence, rather than spiral down the rabbit hole and give in to your fears, rather than become a burden to friends and families around, embrace CBT as a tool to get your mental health in order. Whatever it is you struggle with; be it a phobia, worry, things that you are even ashamed to admit, etc.; you can get help.

One bad thing about some mental health issues is that many do not take note of them until it becomes a problem. Many see it as the way humans are wired. People like this allow their mental health to degenerate until it affects their normal day to day activity and their sanity. It doesn't have to get this bad. You don't have to go deep down the rabbit hole before you get help.

Many people are so used to negative thinking patterns and self-talk. It has eaten so deep into their consciousness that they accept this as a definition of who they are. The problem with not challenging these thoughts is that you receive them and allow them to dictate how you live your life, even holding you back from achieving your potential. If you give up on yourself and do not believe in yourself, how do you expect others to?

The good news I bring is that it doesn't have to be so. You can consciously bring about the change you want in yourself. When the thoughts and emotions come at you with all their force, you feel powerless, a slave to your horrible mental images. Cognitive Behavioral Therapy, however, empowers you with the needed weapon to bring about the change. Never again will you feel powerless under the influence of negative emotions and mental images. The days of being a helpless victim to negative mental health disorders are gone.

Since this is a self-help CBT process, you are the therapist who enforces the healing process. You can heal and be actively involved in the healing process. You can set your goals, define boundaries, and measure your success. This book will equip you with so much, that by the time you are done; you will come out as a new and a transformed being.

The CBT tips provided on the pages of this book are techniques that have been tested. They are tips which have worked within the four walls of a therapist office. We are not presenting to you some hypothesis that only works in theory

You are no longer a helpless slave to your thoughts and emotions, but its master. You can actively decide on the thoughts to dwell on and in turn, form essential characters. We will also explore how powerful meditation can be when combined with cognitive behavioral therapy. These two, when practiced together will produce a tremendous result and fast track your progress.

You can get your mental health back in order today. Take time to go through the teachings in this manual and follow it judiciously. Be excited as you prepare for the delightful turn around that your life will take!

Chapter 1:
Understanding the Basics of CBT

Cognitive Behavioral Therapy, commonly known as CBT, is an attempt to provide a short-term practical approach to solving a psychological problem. It is goal-oriented psychotherapy which attempts to challenge and change people's thought patterns that are responsible for their negative habits or behaviors. Once these thought patterns are disputed, there will be a tremendous improvement in how the victim feels. CBT aims to change the attitude and behavior of people by analyzing beliefs, thoughts, attitudes, etc. that have become part of the person, as well as how it affects the person's behavior.

Cognitive Behavioral Therapy stands out as a means of treating an emotional problem in that it is usually short. With a CBT therapist, most clients have at most one session per week, which last less than an hour. During this period, the client and therapist will work together to get to the root of the problem and come up with helpful strategies to tackle them.

It is helpful to see Cognitive Behavioral Therapy as a combination of behavioral therapy and psychotherapy:

Psychotherapy aims to analyze how authentic the personal meaning is that we have attached to things, situations, and events as well as our thought patterns from childhood.

Behavioral therapy, on the other hand, explores the relationship between our problem, behavior, and response via thoughts. Since this is usually peculiar to individuals, CBT sessions are generally customized to the specific need of the victim.

Understand, however, that the aim of this manual is to equip you with the needed skills to practice CBT skills on yourself, in the comfort of your home. Hence, we will customize the various CBT techniques, that have been tested with a therapist, to a self CBT process. With this, you have in your hands the right tool to get your mental health in order.

Brief History of Cognitive Behavioral Therapy

Cognitive Behavioral Therapy came up in 1960 by a psychiatrist named Aaron Beck. Aaron, during his analytical sessions, discovered that his patients tend to communicate with themselves in their mind – this was almost like they were having a personal conversation. However, they did not let him in on the dialogue.

He discovered that there is a strong link between thoughts and feelings. According to him, automatic thoughts are thoughts directed by emotions that might spring up suddenly. Aaron discovered that most people hardly notice these thoughts, but they could learn to identify and challenge them. A person feeling upset, for instance, would have negative energy. Hence, to understand and solve this problem, it is essential to identify these thoughts.

Aaron called it Cognitive Therapy since the emphasis is on thinking. However, since there is a link between thoughts and behavior, we now call it Cognitive Behavioral Therapy (CBT). While the balance between the cognitive and behavioral parts differ for various therapy sections, it all comes under the general term Cognitive Behavioral Therapy. Over the years, many people have used science to prove the effectiveness of CBT which has helped to solve many problems, this is not the aim of this manual.

Conditions Cognitive Behavioral Therapy Can Treat

With CBT, one can effectively address the following conditions:

- Anxiety
- Anger issues
- Depression
- Social phobia
- Substance abuse
- Relationship and marital issues
- Post-traumatic stress disorder (PTSD)

- Insomnia
- Hypochondria
- Gambling
- Poor self-esteem
- Obsessive-compulsive disorder (OCD)
- Eating disorders

When CBT Sessions Might Be Unhelpful?

There are situations or categories of people that CBT sessions will not work for. Some examples are:

- Presence of a condition that affects rational thinking – brain injury for instance
- Lack of interest in the process, for instance, failing to do the required homework
- People looking for quick fixes

The Need for Homework in CBT Sessions

To get the most out of CBT sessions, homework is vital. It is often said that only those who do homework benefit the most from CBT sessions.

Retraining Your Brain with Cognitive Behavioral Therapy

The therapist will give the client a weekly task. This will serve as a terrific opportunity to practice what you have learned during the section. Bear in mind that the therapy room is a fantastic spot for learning. However, it is nothing like the real world you live in and spend time in. Hence, the reason for taking what you learned in the sessions and applying it in the real world you encounter daily. This will give you the opportunity to understand and change your thoughts.

For the case of self-help CBT sessions, we will identify assignments as we provide solutions on the pages of this manual. The homework is not to make life difficult for you, but to direct you more on the path of recovery from whatever mental health issue you are dealing with.

For instance, people with social anxiety avoid all forms of social interaction; this category of people will prefer to feel better before taking on any activity that puts them amidst people. With CBT, they are introduced mildly to social events in bits, however.

If the client is willing to try this out, they could agree to do the homework. For instance, call a friend or go to the park with a trusted friend. The progress will be tremendous compared to someone who prefers to talk about the problem without taking a step.

A client with an anger issue, for instance, might have to keep a journal of things that triggered the emotion. Hence, at the next CBT session, he can discuss the thoughts or happenings that surrounded the anger.

With time, the client could have another assignment in the form of exercises to cope with such situations.

How CBT Stands Out from Other Forms of Therapy

The way some therapies take place, the client would have to rely on the therapist. This will be a significant form of the treatment process. Hence, when they run into some error, they call their therapist since they see the therapist as all-knowing. This is not so with Cognitive Behavioral Therapy as the therapy – client relationship stands out.

CBT stands out in that it is more practical and problem focused. Frequently, during the sessions, the therapist will ask for feedback and their views on the progress of the meetings.

Alternatively, as you continue yourself CBT process, you will see an improvement which your family and friends should bear witness.

Other areas in which CBT differs from other psychotherapies are:

It is pragmatic in that it identifies an issue and seeks to proffer solution

It is highly structured as you won't go on and on rambling about your life in general. Instead, you get to address specific issues and set goals to solve them.

It is focused on the present problem which has to do with how you think and act, in a bid to address them rather than digging into your past to resolve past issues

It is collaborative in that you work with your therapist. You will not see your therapist as 'all knowing' who will dictate what to do to you. Instead, you will work together to solve your problem.

How Effective Is Cognitive Behavioral Therapy?

Over the years, CBT has proven to be effective in addressing many emotional disorders. While CBT sessions are usually concise, the effect is long term. CBT is as effective as medications for treating anxiety and depression. CBT, however, is more effective and lasts longer. Besides, people often tend to relapse when the prescription runs out, which could lead to a strong dependence on medication to maintain sanity, unlike CBT.

With CBT, however, many people still see tremendous improvement after a couple of sessions. For instance, 12 sessions of CBT are as active as using drugs to tackle depression for two whole years! In other words, with CBT, you get to see a genuine change that is much more than temporary relief.

It should, however, be emphasized that Cognitive Behavioral Therapy is not a miracle cure. In other words, for the session to be productive, the client must be willing to be helped which will show through consistency, dedication to the sessions, observing assignments, and being open. CBT might not work for everyone. Hence, be careful and realistic with your expectation.

How Can A CBT Course Be Helpful?

A CBT session aims to teach the person the following:

- Better understand mood and feelings

- Challenge wrong assumptions

- Desist from assuming the worst

- Come up with reasonable thinking patterns and interpretation of situations

- Learn to analyze situations and events from another angle

- Learn to accept things (yourself) like they (you) are, rather than how you think they (you) should be

- Deep understanding of one's problem

- Stop feeling you are responsible for everything

- Understand the impact of experience even at the present

- Accepting yourself and others, rather than judge

How Does Cognitive Behavioral Therapy Work?
Cognitive Behavioral Therapy works in a pretty complicated way. There might not be a single explanation to shed light on the working principle of CBT. But generally, there are common grounds to CBT which could be specific to the therapist or client.

However, the main idea is that CBT helps you understand issues and life problems by seeking ways to break them into bits and solve them. Cognitive Behavioral Therapy breaks down the problem to five major areas:

- Situations
- Thoughts
- Emotions
- Physical Feelings
- Actions

CBT revolves around the fact that these five areas are connected. This explains why you're thinking about something will affect how you feel physically and emotionally. This, in turn, will reflect in how you respond to the situation.

Addressing Negative Thoughts

We can either respond to a situation positively or negatively. This, most times, is usually determined by how we think about such a situation

This explains why someone who could not sing at a party will feel bad. He or she will beat himself up, saying things like "I am awful," "I suck at everything I do." etc.

As a result of the singular failed attempt to come up with a beautiful melody, he avoids all avenues to go to a party. Rather, he sits at home and prefers to watch movies rather than engage in any form of social interaction that puts him at the spotlight.

However, in contrast to accepting this negative thought pattern, the person could come to understand that there is a first time for everything. He could learn and understand why his voice failed him in his attempt to sing and be hopeful that such will not repeat itself.

With this positive thought pattern, it takes steps to address your phobia of public speaking and with time, you can get a hang of it.

While this example is simplified, it explains how specific thoughts, feelings, and other physical actions and sensations can leave you trapped in a negative vicious cycle. This can even lead to getting into awful situations that make you feel worse about yourself.

What Cognitive Behavioral Therapy aims to do is to challenge the thoughts that are responsible for such feelings. Hence, it challenges and stops negative thoughts by addressing issues that make you feel bad, worried, or scared. It challenges your unhelpful thought pattern with reality, which improves how you feel.

CBT explains that the way people think can be likened to wearing a pair of glasses. With the pair of glasses on, the person is bound to see the world in a specific way. With CBT, we get to see how these unhelpful thought patterns form the reality many people hold on to, which influences their behavior. Ultimately, we can remove this pair of glasses and allow them to view the world in a pretty positive manner.

All patterns of thinking and behavior that affect reality and a positive outcome are what CBT aims to address. This explains why the mind of a person suffering from depression will have a distorted perception and approach to life. This will make such a person jump to conclusions, blame themselves for everything and overall, have a negative mindset.

People who are adapted to negative thought patterns will automatically start to think this way which could affect their behavior. With Cognitive Behavioral Therapy, they challenge these thoughts and learn to view them with the lens of reality.

Once the individual can address their thought pattern, they get to function healthily. With time, as they acquire valuable skills, they develop a constructive approach to tackling problems. This reduces stress, negative thoughts, and lowers the risk of a bad mood.

A Practical Example: Fear of Crowd

A person with agoraphobia, for instance, is afraid of being outside. This person avoids all forms of public and crowded places where escape could be difficult. As a result, the person avoids the mall, elevator, marketplace, church, etc. altogether. This, most times, might be due to a traumatic experience that has happened to the person before in a crowded place. The victim might have witnessed a terrorist attack or a bank robbery, perhaps in childhood. This person hence stays inside and avoids all forms of a crowded place.

With CBT, they can work together and challenge the unhelpful thinking pattern that has been built over time due to the past negative event. During CBT, he can come up with a line that says: "Because I witnessed a bank robbery, all crowded places are dangerous."

Understanding CBT Sessions

CBT sessions could be private with a therapist, or in a group with others who share the same conditions. It can even be done online.

Ideally, you should meet your CBT therapist for at most 20 times, which could be weekly or fortnightly and each session lasts an average of 45 minutes.

Exposure therapy, on the other hand, lasts long to keep tabs on the progress of your anxiety during the session. The session might take place in:

- The therapists' clinic

- A specific place outside if you have certain fears

- In your house, if you have Obsessive-Compulsive Disorder involving an item at home.

Your CBT therapist could be anyone, a healthcare practitioner for instance trained in Cognitive Behavioral Therapy. This could be a psychiatrist, mental health nurse, or a psychologist.

First Session of CBT

Generally, the main aim of the first couple of sessions will help determine if CBT is the right session for you. The therapist will ask questions about your life, past, and background to ascertain if it is the proper process.

It is important for instance to know if the condition of a person suffering from depression or anxiety is interfering with work, social life, and other relationships. The therapist will also request for past treatments, other events related to the problem, as well as what the client aims to achieve with the procedure.

If it is established that CBT will work for you, the therapist will inform you of what to expect from the process. With this, you get to determine if it is right for you and if it's not, there are other treatment alternatives.

Self-help CBT Session

Once it has been established that CBT is right for you, you can take steps to help yourself. Usually, the first step is to break down the problem into several parts. At times, you might have to keep a journal of your thoughts and behavioral patterns.

Using the lens of reality, you will examine the thoughts, feelings, and behavior. The idea is to determine if they are helpful and realistic or not. You will also examine the effect these thoughts have on you. Finally, with various strategies and techniques that you have in this book, you strategize useful ways to address these unhelpful thought patterns.

Part of the aim is to determine what you can change. When you realize these, you can practice this and apply the changes daily. This is usually in the form of homework, as explained in some sections above.

Addressing fear and anxiety could prove difficult and your therapy will hardly ask you to do anything you are not comfortable with. Besides, since you are having a self CBT process, we recommend taking baby steps. Most times, the client determines the pace of progression of each session.

One of the best parts of CBT is that even after the course is over, you can keep applying the principles in your life. With this, the chances of the symptoms returning are slim.

Online CBT

There are helpful online CBT resources available to everyone. You get to benefit from CBT with little or no contact with a therapist.

Many people are uncomfortable about talking to a therapist about their feelings. These people will find online CBT very helpful. All in all, occasional interaction with a therapist, even in the form of phone calls to keep tabs on your progress is recommended.

Chapter 2:
Establish Your Goals

In whatever endeavor you set out to do, the setting of goals is very critical. This is the yardstick with which you track your progress and see how you are doing. Goals are critical in the CBT process, as well, since it helps to know how you are doing.

As a result, you need to decide what you want. It can either be to eliminate the signs of the ailment or get rid of what is wrong. This can be likened to buying an air freshener to take care of foul odor coming from your toilet versus getting rid of the source of the foul odor.

Cognitive Behavioral Therapy becomes very easy when clients can see the link between what the treatment wants from them (which could be completing their homework, probing their innermost thoughts, and challenging bad emotions) and what they hope to get out of therapy.

Right from the very first CBT session, one of the most important things to note and write down is what you aim to achieve.

Many people are confronted with issues that affect their ability to set the right goal. However, this problem is usually a good starting point for goal creation. The help of a CBT therapist is also invaluable in setting realistic goals. With a qualified therapist, you can sort out your problem and learn how to maintain and change goals as needed.

Often, therapists use a beautiful technique to identify goals – called the magic wand question. The question is usually asked this way: "Assuming you have a magic wand with which you can change things that don't appeal to you and with which you get to make the ideal world for yourself, how will things be different?". With this question, one can identify goals that can help in therapy sessions. Even for your personal CBT session, you can use this approach to set your goals

On setting the ideal goal, it is essential to prioritize your goals. With this, you realize the goals that need the utmost attention. Bear in mind that for maximum result, we recommend that you focus your energy on a single target at a time. This allows you to maximize success rather than being confronted with two or more.

On setting the goal for your CBT therapy, it is essential to know if the goal is something you can change by altering your thinking pattern, your actions, or both. This question can direct you to the crucial steps you can take to see the goal to fruition.

Goal Setting in Cognitive Behavioral Therapy
Why do you feel the need for therapy? It is because you identified a deficiency in your life which can only be addressed through therapy. There is a gap between who you are now and who you should be. Setting

a goal is critical to the success of CBT. Bear in mind that CBT is an interactive process that revolves around focus and structure.

As a result, you need goals for the therapy which you can set with assistance from your therapist. The therapist role is to ensure your goals are relevant and precise. Besides, the therapist ensures that the goals are what you do want, not what you think you want. For Cognitive Behavioral Therapy to be productive, goal setting is paramount because it helps to ensure that healing, change, and recovery are possible, and problems are manageable. Besides, your goals make your problem appear solvable, improving your chances of defeating them.

Since this is a vital part of any Cognitive Behavioral Therapy process, it should be done even before the therapy sessions begin. During the first meeting, your therapist works with you to determine if your goals make sense. Often, in therapy sections, you find people saying things like:

- "I want to be happy."

- "I want to be my normal self."

- "I want to be less anxious and depressed."

Without a doubt, the three goals above are good. They capture what anyone entering therapy might have in mind. The problem with these kinds of goals is that they are neither straightforward nor helpful.

Hence, they might not capture what the client really wants which wouldn't make the therapy session as effective as it should be.

The first goal above is the client's attempt to get ahold of their emotions. The issue with this, however, is that emotions are not stable. They change and most times it is a natural response to your situation or environment. Therefore, it can be near impossible to be happy at all time. Experiencing various emotions that are appropriate to a case is perfectly normal. Everyone desires a happy life which, unfortunately, is not possible, as no one can remain in a happy state permanently. Hence, during CBT sessions goals need to be concrete and objective. It should not be about feelings but about what you can do.

The second goal above, as well, is quite tricky because the client aims to return to some default setting that they had years back. The problem with this is that dwelling in the past will keep us from moving forward with life. As enjoyable and exciting as our experience could be, it is usually better and more helpful to focus on the future and accept things we can change, and which will help us. Hence, to readjust that goal, think about something worthwhile, notable, and enjoyable you did in the past and have stopped. Your goal could be to return to such an activity. For instance, you could be used to waking up as early as 5:00 AM to go for a jog in the past. This helped you so much that you lost weight and you were proud of your figure. You had a sexy bikini body that your husband was proud of. Due to commitments to the family or pressure from work, you could not keep up with this lifestyle. Your goal, in this case, should be having at least 30 minutes of exercise per day, rather than a desire to return to the past life. It could also help to set a goal with which you get to fulfill some values that mean so much to you, that when responding to a recent activity it might not be helpful. In the scenario above, the lady in question could try other useful and healthy ways of losing weight if waking up by 5:00 AM will be uncomfortable. Intermittent fast, healthy eating, cutting calories, etc. are all goals she could set to help her return to her beautiful bikini body. This is a pretty different activity, but the overall aim is the same – getting back the sexy bikini body, thereby making her appealing to her husband.

The third example is difficult as it relates to getting rid of something. However, an important thing about a CBT goal is that it is more about what we aim to achieve or have, and not what we will like to do without. The goal of reducing anxiety should be more about avoiding activities or things that trigger anxiety and depression. Your goal should relate to what you can do without the feeling of anxiety. For CBT goals to be effective, it must be positively framed (doing or getting something) rather than negative (avoiding something).

For CBT goals to be practical, think about the things you value. In setting goals, the idea is to approach something that will help improve your mood and overall life. It should help you connect with important things which will make you better off. Hence, rather than setting goals in the direction of self-critical thinking; for instance, I want to be less fat, try to think about meaningful ways to get that done.

Retraining Your Brain with Cognitive Behavioral Therapy

As soon as you are aware of a goal you will like to work towards in a CBT session, be sure to make it very specific. For instance, you could decide to try out intermittent fasting because you want to lose weight. This is good since it is a means to an end, and it has meaning to you. The problem with this, however, is that it is not specific enough yet. A goal will be:

I will have a 16:8 intermittent fast on Mondays and Thursday for the next month.

The setting of goals for your CBT sessions in this way will spell out exactly what you need to do, how you will get it done, when and where as appropriate. This will make it easy to know when you have achieved your goal. In making your goals specific, we encourage you to think SMART.

By SMART, we mean:

Specific: In other words, no generalization. Let the goal be clear and focused on the exact thing you want. There is a high probability that you will achieve a specific goal, rather than something generalized. In other words, do not say you want to learn how to sing. Be specific about the action you want to take to make this a reality.

Measurable: You should have objective criteria with which you will measure your progress as you attain each goal you set. You should have questions like: How will I know when my goal is met? Still, in the previous example of singing, a goal could be: I will watch two YouTube videos to improve my singing skills. This is both specific and measurable.

Achievable: We mean your goal should be attainable. You should have plans to bring your goals to fruition. Your goals should involve actionable strategies that can help you achieve it. A person who aims to finish the next city marathon race must have plans to make this a reality. In other words, the goal must be complemented with the idea of action, or else, failure is inevitable.

Realistic: Considering your skills, ability, time frame, and resources will your goals be attainable. Yes, it is good to set high goals as it increases motivation. However, when your goals are so lofty that reaching them becomes a burden, you can feel like a failure. All in all, your goal should be in line with reality. Aiming to be the next US president might be foolhardy without adequate preparation and experience in politics.

Timely: Besides having goals that are realistic, achievable, and measurable; you should have a tangible time frame to work with. This keeps you on your toes and helps deal with procrastination. You need to be realistic on how long it will take to see your goal to fruition. Many people, due to impatience give in to frustration when they do not see their goals to fruition. This explains why a person aiming to lose 50 pounds of body fat will have to be patient to see this through with time. It doesn't happen overnight, neither does it come on a platter of gold.

CBT SMART Goal in Action: An Example

Retraining Your Brain with Cognitive Behavioral Therapy

Still on the illustration of a lady in her mid-thirties, who was once appealing to her husband. She is now so busy at work and the demands of keeping up with family needs do not give her the time to wake up early for a jog.

She might come up to lose weight as thus:

Specific: I want to have 10 minutes of sit-ups every morning.

Measurable: I will have a journal to record my progress on this.

Achievable: I will wake early so I can be faithful to it.

Realistic: I should be able to spare ten minutes every day. That is realistic and not too much. It is just for ten minutes. Hence, it will not affect my commitment to work and family.

Timely: I will do this thrice a week, and then my husband will assess me after a month to see if I am achieving progress.

The SMART approach to set goals can be a simple yet effective method to have a concise goal and a plan to work with.

All in all, having a SMART goal can be challenging but it is possible. With the help of the principles discussed here, you can set a useful goal for yourself. Besides, applying the SMART principle above will tremendously increase the chances of having successful goals.

Chapter 3:
Understanding Cognitive Distortion

As humans, we are wired to trust our brain, which is how it should be. It is your brain, it wants the best for you; hence, trusting it is rational!

This is good because the brain by default is wired to keep us safe, direct us towards what is good for us, and help us solve what we come across in our daily interactions with people.

There are, however, sometimes when your brain might not be very helpful. No, we do not mean that your brain is lying to you on purpose. But it has developed some faulty and questionable properties over the course of time.

It will surprise you how easy it is for faulty wirings to develop in the brain. This is because the way the brain is wired, it tends to find a link between thoughts, ideas, actions, consequences, and events whether they are linked or not.

This is the foundation of common issues that humans have nowadays – the tendency to connect things where truly, there is none. Hence, the brain assumes that since two variables are related, one must be as a result of the other. This is false since correlation is not always the same as causation.

It is easy for the brain to analyze a complicated or coincidental event and come up with false and unrealistic assumptions. This is the same way it is easy to link two happenings that coincide even though there is no real relationship between them.

The world of psychology has coined a lot of terms for this brain error. However, looking at this in the context of our thoughts and beliefs, it is known as cognitive distortion

Explaining Cognitive Distortions

Just as the name implies, cognitive distortions can be interpreted as a distortion or error or fault in cognition or thinking or understanding. In other words, cognitive distortions are a faulty interpretation of ourselves and the world around us. These are irrational thoughts and ideas that we allow to take root and reinforce with time.

These thinking patterns, most times, are tough to notice – you hardly recognize them because they are already part of your daily thoughts. Therefore, the effect on the victim is usually bad since changing what you don't know can be hard.

There are various forms of cognitive distortion. However, they all have some things in common because:

- Patterns or ways of thinking and seeing things

- Which are not true

- And can result in psychological damage

Many at times, it is usually difficult for people to admit to false thinking patterns. Such victims might think it is impossible for them to be controlled by any irrational beliefs. Although not everyone is a victim of these distorted thinking patterns, everyone in one way or the other have some form of distortion.

The fact that you are human has qualified you for one of the various cognitive distortions which could have happened at any time in the course of your existence. The ability to recognize, challenge, and modify these faulty thought patterns marks the difference between those that are long-term victims and people who struggle with it occasionally. This is just like any life skill in which some have mastered while others have not.

Cognitive distortion has been shown to form a large part of the symptoms of depression and anxiety. In other words, cognitive distortion comes with the tendency of depression and anxiety (Nancy Schimelpfening, 2018)

This faulty thinking pattern, also known as cognitive distortion, is one of the primary ingredients that trigger depression (after all it comes up as a result of wrong assumptions in thoughts). Although, it has not been defined if these false ideas are a direct cause of depression or vice versa. However, one clear thing is that they do go hand in hand.

A List of The Most Common Cognitive Distortions

Cognitive distortion was popularized and made known via extensive research conducted by two researchers (David Burns and Aaron Beck.) It was research in the field of psychotherapy and psychiatry.

Mental Filtering

Someone suffering from mental filtering will only capitalize on the negative details of an event. The person will be so concerned about the negative aspects of an event that the positive parts leave no impact. This explains why a person who had a little flaw in a presentation but was still able to close the deal would be so disturbed by the flaw that they won't celebrate. Their victory is nothing as it has been affected by the flaw.

Another instance is a married couple where the husband cheated. The wife now dwells on this act of infidelity, feels the marriage is worthless and questions the years of faithfulness of the man.

Polarized Thinking

Also known as black and white thinking, this person sees situations as either black or white, an all or nothing thinking mentality. To this person, humans or things either must be perfect or a complete failure, no middle ground exists. This person sees things only at the extreme – either fantastic or awful.

Overgeneralization

This is the distortion that allows a person to have an overall conclusion based on a single incident. This explains why a person who survived an airplane will do all in his or her capacity to stay away from air travel. As a result of something terrible that once happened, they expect this to be the norm. This person assumes that an unpleasant event forms a pattern, or a cycle of defeat meant to keep repeating.

For instance, a person who went off key while singing to a congregation concludes he is a horrible singer and should never try singing again!

Jumping to Conclusions – Mind Reading

People in this category assume what the other person is thinking even without the person telling them. They claim to know why the other person is acting the way they are. Without a doubt, it is possible to know what others are thinking. However, this distortion often manifests itself in negative things that people believe.

Your friend walks in with a frown and your imagination tells you she's got a piece of bad news for you, is an example of this.

Jumping to Conclusions – Fortune Telling

Related to mind reading is the fortune telling aspect. This is when people make conclusions based on little shreds of evidence and believes in them so much that it dictates the person's life.

A perfect example is a job seeker who believes no company is willing to hire him because five years after graduation, he has no job still. He has no way of knowing how his life will turn out. He, however, believes this prediction and holds it as a truth rather than a possibility.

Magnification or Minimization

Also referred to as catastrophizing, this person is always expecting calamities or negatives in all situations. This distortion could either be two sides of an extreme as the person amplifies the meaning of things or minimizes it.

The person employs 'what if' questions to think about the worst situations. For instance, he hears about an accident and assumes it could have happened to him. This person elaborates the importance of molecular events like their error.

On the other extreme, they see or label essential things until they appear insignificant like the imperfection of others.

Personalization

This distortion makes the victim believe that what others do or say is related to them directly. Even something that has no link with the person will be taken personally. This person also tends to have an unhealthy comparison with others to see who is more successful or smarter.

This person also tends to take the blame for something unpleasant that happened which has no direct relation to them. For instance, "If I had not left home, the cat wouldn't have wandered away and got killed by a vehicle. If only I had been at home, this wouldn't have happened."

Control Fallacies

This type of cognitive distortion can be seen in either of two ways:

That our lives are being controlled by some forces such as fate, hence we must accept what life throws at us helplessly.

That we have total control of our life and surroundings, hence we are responsible for all that happens around us.

These two beliefs are faulty and equally damaging. No one, in this universe, does not have any control over all that happens in their life and around them. In the same manner, no one is in total control of all that happens. Even in situations like examinations where your grade depends on your tutor, you have some indirect control in terms of your preparation for the exam.

Fallacy of Fairness

The ideal world would be a fair one in which everyone is happy. This, however, is far from reality which could trigger negative feelings when this person is faced with the wrong side of life. We have all heard the saying that Life is not fair, and things might not always go our way.

This person, however, lives life with the assumption that everything that happens should be judged based on a perceived fairness rule. Things will not always go as wanted or the way it should. This could lead to a feeling of anger or resentment when it does happen.

Blaming

This could be two sides of a coin. A person engaged in this kind of cognitive distortion believes others are the cause of their emotional trauma. He could also take it upon himself and assume responsibility for every negative occurrence, even things outside his control.

For instance, consider the statement: "Stop making me upset!" This is wrong in that no one can dictate how we feel as our emotions and emotional reaction is our sole responsibility.

Fallacy of Change

Also, in the class of cognitive distortion relating to fallacy is the fallacy of change. With this, people expect others to change when we encourage, advise, or force them to. This person holds on to the belief that they can only be happy and fulfilled if they succeed in changing others.

This distortion is often seen in a relationship. For instance, a parent who thinks: "if I can only get my kid to stop keeping bad friends, I will be a happy parent" has the fallacy of change distortion.

Should Statements

Also, in the class of damaging cognitive distortion are should statements. This is a statement of what you think you "should" do, or what your "ought" to do and in some cases as well, what you "must" do. They are not always personal as they apply to others as well which happens by having expectations, we feel others must meet.

Holding too much to should statements often imposes a set of unrealistic expectations. We usually end up miserable due to the inability to meet up with this expectation. In the same manner, holding this belief (should statements) about others often causes disappointment and frustration when others do not meet expectations.

Emotional Reasoning

A person experiencing this kind of cognitive distortion assumes their feeling to be fact and believes them. Hence, this person accepts their feeling as an automatic truth. In other words, a person feeling sad must be depressed.

Humans generally are ruled by emotions which are usually active in many people and can blind their rational thoughts and reasoning. This happens when a person allows himself to be governed by emotions, without interest in what logic or fact has to say. As a result, people in this category believe that everything reflects what their feelings dictate to them. It is what I am feeling, and it is true!

Always Being Right

I bet people with perfectionist syndrome will identify with this distortion. This person is ruled by the belief that we must either be right and accurate. To this person, that a person is wrong is entirely unacceptable. Hence, he would argue with his last breath to prove that he is right.

This is common in online forums where people spend hours debating over religious or political issues. They will go far beyond the point where reasonable humans will. These people do not accept the argument as a difference of opinion, rather an intellectual battle that must be won. This person prioritizes the feeling of being right to another people's opinion.

Disqualifying the Positive

With this, the person, even though they acknowledge positive events, will not embrace them. Even in the face of glaring positive experiences, this person will engage in negative, distorted thought patterns.

For instance, a class of students that was positively acknowledged as good performance on a test might reject the accolade. They could attribute the positive review to the teacher just not wanting to talk about the misbehavior of their students.

Global Labeling

Also referred to as mislabeling, this person, in the event of one or two happenings comes to a general conclusion about themselves or other people. This is overgeneralization in its extreme. Hence, the person will not acknowledge an error in a context; instead, he would come to a universal conclusion to themselves or others.

Such a person might attribute himself as a loser in a situation where he failed at what he ought to do. Also, when another person's behavior affects someone negatively, such a person, without a perfect understanding of the situation around the context might conclude that the person is awful.

With mislabeling, people tend to attribute heavy language with huge emotional meaning to an event. For instance, a person with this type of cognitive disorder would not say that someone hired house help. Instead, he would say they invited strangers into their home.

Heaven's Reward Fallacy

This final distortion is a pretty popular one. It involves people believing that some unseen forces are keeping records of their sacrifice, struggles, hard works, and self-denial which will eventually pay off. This type of thinking is distorted as there are many instances which we could all point to in our personal life where sacrifices and hard work did not pay off.

There are times that things don't go how we want regardless of our input and sacrifice. To however think otherwise is pretty damaging which could trigger disappointments, bitterness, resentment, and frustration and at times depression when the expected reward fails to show up.

In Conclusion

The entirety of these various cognitive distortions originates from the thoughts. Our way of thinking alongside our interpretation of the world influences our feeling which triggers multiple types of emotions. With these emotions, we judge and interpret life experiences.

Our judgments, without a doubt, often vary and are at times not accurate. This gives us a biased interpretation of the world and blinds us from seeing the world and events in it how they really are, instead, we see things based on how we are. Without a doubt, how we are is a factor of our interpretation of the world and general happenings in it. This goes back to the thought we have allowed.

By working on these cognitive distortions, you can take charge of those thoughts. The next chapter will shed light on these.

Chapter 4:
Break the Cycle of Negative Thoughts

One of the many applications of Cognitive Behavioral Therapy is in fixing negative thoughts. With the help of a therapist, such people can replace negative thinking patterns with pretty positive ones. The singular act of changing the thinking pattern can help improve one's mental outlook. This leads to a more positive attitude, improved behavior, and better relationships. Many times, people that have suffered some trauma in childhood or the past are likely to experience negative thinking patterns. With CBT, they can realign these thinking patterns which can help create a better future. With CBT, the negative thought patterns that trigger anxiety and depression can be reprogrammed.

When we have distorted thoughts, we suffer in one way or the other. At times, this happens during upsetting events in our life such as a disagreement in a relationship, poor grade in school, issues at work, etc. The way we think about these events brings about negativity which ends up dictating our mood. Although the act of feeling bad might be necessary for people to learn from their errors, many are lost in a deep and unhealthy hole of this bad feeling.

What is Healthy Thinking and How Does CBT Help?

With good thinking, you get to understand how your thoughts – helpful and harmful ideas, affect your feelings and actions. You can consciously learn how to employ the power of the right-thinking pattern to better your life.

Getting rid of negative thoughts might be the ticket to healthy living as well as victory to life challenges. It can help manage stress and deal with many mental health issues like depression, sleep problem, and anxiety.

With CBT, you can reconfigure your thinking pattern towards a positive way. You can either work with a therapist or employ the techniques discussed below to improve yourself.

CBT will restructure your thinking pattern in such a way that good thoughts become part of you naturally. For instance, you might be upset about a grade in one of your courses where you narrowly crossed the pass mark. While you passed other courses as well, but this one course dampened your mood such that you felt down and defeated. You might even think you are a failure who knows nothing.

One of the many examples of negative thinking patterns is capitalizing on bad instances. With time, you can train yourself to watch out for such negative thinking patterns and combat them with reality.

You can realize that the horrible things you say to yourself affect your productivity and keep you from the functional aspect of your life and work. CBT focuses on using several techniques to help refine your thinking pattern:

- You can detect negative thoughts that you have

- You can put an end to those thoughts

- You can focus on positive thoughts as a replacement to the negative ones

- You can challenge evil thoughts with facts

- You can question negative conclusions about yourself

Fixing Faulty Thinking Patterns

We have presented a lot of useful methods in here that you can use to challenge irrational and automatic negative thoughts. Since people differ, what will fix your negative thinking pattern differs from what will fix another's'. Therefore, attempt a couple of them and consider the one that works best.

Identify the Negative Thinking Pattern

The first and most important step in fixing any issue is in knowing what it is, exactly. It doesn't stop here; you have got to understand how deep the root of the problem has gone. It can be likened to fixing a vehicle in which the auto mechanic has to perform some diagnostic to determine what is wrong.

Therefore, you should identify and keep tabs on the type of cognitive distortion that affects you daily, even before trying to fix them. In a day, have a list where you write down these thoughts as they pop in your head. When you have a real list, you can judge this list in relation to the type of cognitive distortion we discussed in the previous chapter.

Analysis of your thinking pattern helps you see the distortion that has eaten deep into your life. This method gives you the capacity to address each problem in a pretty natural way. Besides using a journal, there are apps with which you can keep tabs on your cognitive distortion.

Analyze the Evidence

You will have to do this the same way a judge gives an unbiased trial of an event. To be successful with this step, you need to remove yourself from the upsetting event or distorted thinking. This will allow you to give the evidence a critical, unbiased, and objective examination. With this, you can recognize the basis for your cognitive distortion. A person who has agoraphobia because of a failed attempt to sing at a party should consider events where he was excellent during friends, for instance.

A proven way to analyze the evidence is to consider each thought that leads to the events. After this, you then decide if those thoughts are just a shred of opinion or a fact. For instance, statements like "I am lazy" and "People do not like me" are mere opinions. "I did not prepare well for the test" and "I did not take care of the cat before leaving" on the other hand are facts.

When you distinguish facts from opinion, you get to understand which one's form part of the negative thinking (which is usually the opinions). With this, you direct your efforts to correct them.

Combating the Double Standard Method

Rather than engaging in harsh and demeaning self-talk, we can try the alternative which is to talk to ourselves in a caring and friendly way, like we would to a friend. Generally, humans tend to be harder on themselves compared to others we care about. The way we castigate ourselves in our mind, we wouldn't do that to a friend.

Avoid treating yourself with a standard higher than you treat everyone. We recommend using a single standard for all, including you. This is fair and healthy compared to the double standard method. Encourage yourself, just like you would encourage a friend if they fall short of expectation.

A person that had a lot of broken relationships might have negative thoughts like: "he is eventually going to leave you," or "You will soon do something to screw this up again." However, you can counter such automatic thoughts with a pretty positive response for instance, "I have learned from my past mistakes" or "I am a terrific addition to any man's life."

Shades of Gray Thinking

Our mind has been used to taking the easy way out when it comes to thinking and processing information to hasten our decision-making process. As a result, combating black and white thought could be challenging. While this thinking pattern could be good at times, it subjects the person to hold on to irrational beliefs as well.

To combat thinking in shades of gray, you will have to evaluate an event on a scale of 0 through 100. When you fall short of an expectation, look at it as a partial success on the scale and not a complete failure.

For instance, someone might think, "I am just so useless. I could not wake up early to have my morning sit up exercise today." How will a single failed morning of missing your sit-up routine thwart your effort of losing fat? Something you have been so faithful to, for weeks! Analyzing this acclaimed failure on a scale of 0 to 100, it could be a 3% likelihood.

Consciously Practice Positive Thinking

It is not a coincidence – Successful people in life do expect success and practice a positive attitude. Even with setbacks, they do not allow it to get to them and they have formed a habit of seeing the bright side in all situations. Bear in mind that no one is a failure; it is just a consequence of our action. If the result does not appeal to you, try and practice positive thinking.

You might be preparing for a presentation and you fell asleep. Instead of feeling awful after waking up, think of many positive things instantly. For example, I am relaxed and energized, my brain is fresh and in top condition to perform excellently, etc. Consciously try to redirect your thoughts to positive ones, rather than castigate yourself at your failed attempt to stay up and practice.

See Disappointments as Normal

You might not be able to do without disappointments; hence, do not beat yourself up. Your reaction to what life throws at you has a significant role to play in your overall wellbeing and happiness. Many people are so immersed in their past failures that they fail to believe in themselves. This has led them to negative thinking and behaviors. While we encourage you to feel the disappointments, do not get stuck in it.

For your wellbeing, know the difference between things you can control and those you cannot. Be sure to imbibe the habit of letting go of things you have no control over. Your fiancé cheated on you even though you have been a good and faithful partner. Yes, mourn the infidelity and make yourself available for the next faithful man, rather than thinking something is wrong with you.

Try the Experimental Method

Most of the thoughts that give people problems are usually irrational. Hence, you can test your thoughts to see if they have any solid basis.

For instance, you have always wanted to lose weight by intermittent fasting. But the idea of going without food scares the hell out of you and you assume it is "too hard" hence you cannot just do it. However, intermittent fasting doesn't have to be extended. You can eat your first meal at 9 am and the next one at 6 pm. With time, as you progress, you can increase the duration of the fast. Now that doesn't sound as impossible as your mind has made you believe right?

Also, consider a person who believes she can never win a marathon race since she has never run a long distance before. This person can test whether this is true or not. What if he runs 1 km at a time and increases the distance gradually? While this might take time, she will realize that she can run the marathon race.

Survey Method
Just like the experimental method, the survey method is focused on using the experience of others in similar situations to judge ours. With their response, we can accept our thoughts as valid or not.

For instance, someone might hold on to the opinion that "wives are obligated to share in the financial responsibility of running a home." They could contact a couple of friends who are happily married and seem to be doing fine. This person will soon realize that not all wives assist their husband financially and they still have a blossoming relationship.

For you to ascertain the authenticity and rationality of your thoughts, you can talk to a couple of friends and examine their experience.

Have Time for Daily Positive Activities

Another interesting CBT technique to counter negative thought is to give time for a positive activity in your daily schedule. It doesn't have to be something elaborate and can be as short as 10 minutes. It could be going for a walk and listening to the birds sing as fresh air caresses your skin, listening to your favorite band, watching a comedy series. With this, you have something to look forward to, recharge yourself, and break the cycle of negative thoughts.

For a week, have a journal where you keep a list of healthy activities that appeal to you or something that makes you fulfilled. With this, you get to relieve stress and build the foundation for positive thoughts in your brain.

Apply the Semantic Method

People who are fond of castigating themselves with should statements ("I should do this and that") are judging themselves with a set of rules which has no basis. Should statements be like a judgment about you or someone else that has no base and are plainly unhelpful.

Hence, whenever you are tempted to use a "should statement," try something different. For instance: "It would be nice if..." This statement, asides from being different semantically, is more pleasant to the ears. It can make you look at the world and its events in a pretty positive way.

Shouldn't I wake up early?

Wouldn't it be nice if I woke up early?

The first statement will trigger guilt and make you feel bad about yourself. While the other statement makes you curiously examine the thought, making you open to receiving the underlying idea.

Definitions

This is a good CBT method of combating irrational ways that people who like to argue will find helpful. For instance, what does it mean to define someone as a failure? A fool? Or a nonentity? A careful assessment of this alongside some global labels might show that it has to do with specific behaviors and not the overall individual.

With the above in mind, analyzing a label and asking a clarifying question about the meaning we give to them will daze you. For instance, what does it mean to label someone as a failure? Failure at what? At singing or cooking? Has she really learned how to cook? What is her experience with cuisine? The more you challenge an assertion or label with clarifying questions, the more you realize how valid or accurate, such label is.

Understanding Reattribution

With cognitive distortion that involves personalization and blaming, the person takes responsibility for all that happens to them, irrespective of the actual cause.

What reattribution aims to accomplish is to shed light on external factors, as well as, input from others that led to the issue. No matter how someone takes the blame for a problem, it is a waste of energy. However, such energy can be channeled to resolve the issue rather than pass blame. Assigning responsibility is different from avoiding blame, but rather, it involves making sure you do not beat yourself up for something not entirely your fault.

For instance, one of your kids has always been a headache. No matter what you do, this kid does not fail to disappoint you. You are not to blame entirely for the way the child chose to live his life. This is because training him was the responsibility of you and your husband, and it was his choice to listen to the training. Hence, your share of the blame is 33.33% going by the analysis above. It is not entirely your fault.

You can learn to break the cycle of negative thoughts, either on your own or with your therapist. Since the pattern of negative thinking differs, the entire list above will not apply to everyone. You can, however, choose the ones that relate to you and use them to counter your faulty patterns of thinking.

You must have noticed in the course of the chapters there are exercises in the form of assignments because the real healing takes place outside the wall of a therapist clinic. Healing takes place when you practice what you learn. These are essential things you must do to record improvement in your thinking pattern and get back your mental health.

Chapter 5:
Understanding Depression

Nothing seems to interest you anymore. Even the activities that gave you pleasure now irritate you and finding the zeal to do what you ought to do seems so tricky.

Many people can recognize the symptoms of depression since they feel down. However, periods of depression can be said to be normal especially when a person faces a horrible life and personal issues like the sudden loss of a job and divorce or breakup. The problem starts when the person refuses to snap out of this low state weeks after the event.

There are many things responsible for depression. Studies affirm that environmental and biological factors are often tools that contribute to depression. Also, genetic factors are also primal to the onset of depression. Science has revealed the vital role several chemicals, like serotonin, play in the brain. In a likewise manner, when a person suffers a severe traumatic event or an in-depth emotional breakdown in the past, the risk of depression is high.

What Is Depression?

Unlike sadness, depression is one of the most common mental illnesses that affect millions of people. It is classified as depression because of the nature and duration. A person can only be said to suffer from depression if five out of nine symptoms are present for over two weeks. Most common symptoms are deep sadness and a general disinterest in things that would typically excite the person.

Records have it that women are more prone to depression than men. (Nancy Schimelpfening, 2019) This is as a result of the various changes in hormones that occur during their lifespan. (Claudio et al, 2008) Besides, it is crucial to note that the high depression rate recorded in women might be attributed to the fact that women, unlike men are more likely and encouraged to discuss their feelings.

While it is common to women, it affects men and women alike. The World Health Organization has it that around 350 million people all over the world suffer from depression. (Christian Nordqvist, 2012) This means for every seven people, one person must have an episode of depression in their life.

Senior citizens are also more likely to experience depression. Older people with little social supports battling with an illness make this age group more prone to depression.

Worthy of note is the fact that not all loss of interest and depressive episodes can be passed off as a mental disorder. Humans are bound to experience unstable emotions and have periods of sadness at times.

Depression stands out in that it is difficult to overcome, which has no relation to defects or personal weakness. It is a horrible mental disorder which people of all age and class suffers from. Over 50% of people battling with depression do not function in society well. This is often characterized by staying away from social places or places of obligation like schools or work, poor interaction with family members, etc.

Symptoms of Depression

It should be noted that sadness is a minute part of depression. Some people with depression might not feel sad. There are many other symptoms of depression. Depression is so horrible that it affects not only the feelings but can dictate one's behaviors. Hence, we classify the signs under the psychological, behavioral, and psychotic subheadings.

Experiencing any combination of the following for at least two weeks might be a pointer to depression.

- Being filled with self-blame

- Loss of self-respect and worthlessness

- A depressed mood that brings a feeling of sadness and hopelessness

- Unexplainable tiredness and loss of passion and strength

- Continuous anxiousness and emptiness

- Problem with concentration and deciding

- Behavioral symptoms:

- Very low productivity with decreased energy

- Suicidal tendencies/thoughts

- Sudden lack of interest in fun and general activities

- Social withdrawal

- Emotional episodes like crying

- Changes in appetite

- Irritability and restlessness

Psychotic Symptoms:

In some cases of depression, like 10 to 15%, the person has a false sense of reality. This will be psychotic depression and the person suffers from incorrect thoughts. Many times, these thoughts usually complement the depressed mood – this person will be affected by life failures and shortcomings such as guilt and death.

Causes of Depression

Depression, many times is a combination of several factors. Hence, it is challenging to attribute a specific element to the cause of depression. Some of these are:

Retraining Your Brain with Cognitive Behavioral Therapy

Biochemical factors: According to research, depression is often caused by an imbalance of some chemicals in the brain like serotonin, norepinephrine, and growth factors such as BDNF, etc. (Anita E., 2012) Although, more research into this has shown that depression is more than the depreciation of some brain chemicals. However, a recent study has passed depression as a result of a noted pattern in brain activities and the way some areas of the brain interact.

Psychosocial factors: Also, depression can arise as a result of significant life events such as loss of a friend or relative, promotion, loss of a job, bad grades, etc. These are life events that can trigger so much pressure, tension and stress that the body will find it difficult to handle.

This kind of the depressive episode can be managed with a healthy social life. A stable relationship, the presence of supportive friends and loved ones around, secured job, etc. can give the person a form of safety which will enhance stability and structure.

Biogenetic factors: At times, depression might run in the bloodline. This explains why kids of parents with depression are more prone to having depression unlike kids of parents who do not have depression.

Light: This type of depression is known as Seasonal Affective Disorder which is a form of depression that has to do with reduced daylight. It is often triggered by a deficiency of sunlight, hence, can be treated by light therapy.

Childhood Trauma: devastating events that occurred in childhood like rape, abuse, or the loss of a parent can trigger brain changes. This can increase the likelihood of depression. Also, attempting to block out thoughts and events from the past, traumatic childhood events could trigger depression.

Understanding the Various Types of Depression

Depression comes in various forms, which could be mild or severe. Depression can be severe or short spanned. There are also circumstances that can trigger depression.

An understanding of the form of depression is an excellent way to know the type of treatment to expect. Besides, people already with depression need to have facts about their specific depression for them to get help. Some of the types of depression are:

Major Depressive Disorder

Also known as clinical depression or major depression, it is a pretty common form of depression which is particular to women. Over 16 million Americans in a year had this type of depression in 2015. (ADAA) For someone to be diagnosed with major depressive disorder, the person must have at least five symptoms which persist for two or more weeks, according to the American Psychiatric Association. The symptoms can be any of emptiness, worthlessness, sadness, guilt, weariness, loss of appetite, guilt, changes in sleeping pattern, etc.

Clinical depression comes in two types, which are the "atypical depression" and "melancholic depression." People with a regular depression sleep and overeat, in addition to being anxious and very reactive. People with melancholic depression, on the other hand, do have issues with sleep as they are laden with thoughts of guilt.

Treatment-Resistant Depression

There are times people with major depressive disorder do not respond to treatment. With one and many more antidepressants, they show no tangible improvement. This could be as a result of environmental and genetic depression.

To help people with treatment-resistant depression, there must be a proper diagnosis to identify the other causes which could be medical or psychiatric.

Subsyndromal Depression

A person is said to be "subsyndromal" if the person suffers major depression but does not have all the qualities for the diagnosis of depression. This person might have three or four symptoms, rather than five.

Persistent Depressive Disorder

People suffering from a persistent depressive disorder (PDD) have a sad and low mood with at least two symptoms of depression lasting two years or more. For kids and teens, if the symptoms of depression or irritability last for a year, they could be passed off as having PDD.

For someone to be diagnosed with persistent depressive disorder, there should be one or more of the following: sleep issues (excessive or inadequate); low self-esteem, poor concentration, fatigue, and feeling of hopelessness.

Premenstrual Dysphoric Disorder

This is usually common in women of childbearing age. In the week before a woman's period, she could experience symptoms like sadness, anxiety, irritability, and depression. This is common in 10% of all women in childbearing age.

This is because such women are abnormally sensitive to hormonal changes during their cycle.

Bipolar Depression

This is characterized by severe mood swings and energy, from euphoria to feeling blue, etc. Also called bipolar disorder, victims usually show at least a sign of mania. It is common in young adults and affects men and women equally. Although, studies reveal that men are more prone to maniac behavior while women are more susceptible to the depressive symptoms.

Without treatment, it worsens, although there is a treatment option available.

Disruptive Mood Dysregulation Disorder

This is a type of depression common in kids that have a problem regulating their emotions. With these, they throw tantrums and scream without cause. They are prone to being irritable, always in a foul mood and causing trouble with their mates and teachers.

The issue with these kids is that their emotional outburst is so loud that they cannot contain it. Hence, their actions are based on what they feel. It can be treated with psychotherapy and medication.

Postpartum (Or Perinatal) Depression

Having childbirth should be a huge source of joy to the parents. At times, however, it could trigger postpartum depression (PPD). This affects 25% of women and 13% of men. For women, this type of depression is caused by fluctuations in hormones, fatigue, and others. For men, on the other hand, it is caused by changing roles and lifestyle adjustment associated with parenting.

While postpartum depression can occur as soon as a newborn arrives, it can also happen any time after the first year of the childbirth. This is often characterized by a feeling of exhaustion, great sadness, and being overwhelmed which affects daily activities. It could make some people want to hurt themselves or the baby.

Seasonal Affective Disorder

Also known as seasonal depression. Seasonal affective disorder is a depression that recurs and comes around during the winter or fall. It is accompanied by a change in mood which results in low energy.

Victims, often, are prone to withdrawal from social activities, excessive eating and sleeping, excessive carbs and sugary things which ultimately lead to weight gain.

There is a tendency that Seasonal affective disorder runs in the family, although women and young adults have a higher risk factor. The exact cause is not known, although research speculates that it could be due to an imbalance of serotonin in the brain. Excessive sleep hormone, as well as depleted levels of the D Vitamin, could be a factor.

Psychotic Depression

Victims in this category have depression that has to do with psychosis (losing touch with reality.) Victims are prone to delusions (holding on to wrong facts) as well as hallucinations (hearing and seeing things that are not real.)

Cognitive Theories of Depression

Cognitive behavioral theories, also known as cognitive theories, deal with mental events such as thoughts and feelings. We refer to them as "cognitive behavioral" since they deal with mental events concerning learning. Today, cognitive behaviorism is gradually gaining popularity because it is the framework of the most dominant and well-known psychotherapy form available today called Cognitive Behavioral Therapy.

According to Cognitive Behavioral Theory, depression arises due to poor adaptation, faulty learning that occurs through biased and untrue thoughts. It is possible to learn depressive cognition, for instance, the case of kids in a defective family taking note of how their parents fail to handle stressful life experiences successfully.

The cognitive theory of depression explains that the pattern of thinking of depressed people is different. It is this irregular thinking pattern that facilitates depression. This tells why a depressed person has a cynical and pessimistic view of themselves, the environment, and the future. This also affects the way they process facts as it tends to be negative, as well as taking responsibility for bad occurrences. The negative thought pattern triggers a negative bias which makes it easy for depressed people to process bad situations more than needed, making such people prone to developing depression as a response to stress and stressful occurrences.

Aaron Beck's Cognitive Theory of Depression

Many Cognitive Behavioral Theorists have come up with their definition of how cognition relates to thoughts. Dr. Aaron Beck revealed that most people experience symptoms of depression as a result of dysfunctional and false beliefs. Also, there is a link between how serious someone's negative thought is and how deep the rabbit hole of their depression is. In simple terms, one is more likely to experience depression with abundant negative thoughts.

Aaron revealed that depressed people are usually dominated by three major false beliefs:

- I am defective and not complete

- I can never succeed with anything

- No hope for my future

These three are described as the negative cognitive triads which could trigger depression if someone accommodates such thoughts.

An instance of the negative cognitive trial will help understand how people become depressed. Let's assume that after three years in a relationship, you just had a breakup. If you do not know how to put the negative cognitive triad under control, you will likely falsely assume that this unfortunate event is because of a personal fault. You will be faced with thoughts of doubting yourself and with the idea that your partner left you because you are unworthy.

As your thought process is controlled by the negative cognitive trial, you will conclude that you are a failure. With these conclusions, depression sets in. On the other hand, if you can break the grip of the negative triad beliefs, you will not take the blame for the breakup and wallow in guilt and regrets for too long. You will likely pick yourself up after a month or two and get back in the market for other potential suitors.

Besides the fact that dysfunctional thoughts are negative, holding on to such beliefs can shape what you focus on. This explains why people that are depressed only concentrate on parts of their environment that confirm their irrational thoughts and false beliefs. This happens even if there is proof to contradict such erroneous belief right before them.

This failure to pay adequate attention to what will liberate them is called faulty information processing.

Many depressed people suffer from faulty information processing. As a result, someone depressed will likely pay attention to a piece of information which correlates their contrary belief and expectation, while they intentional block out pieces of evidence that counteract those facts.

Such people, assuming they have a dinner party to plan, they will be on the lookout for the casserole that was burnt. They will forget all other aspects of the party that went smoothly. These people have the habit of exaggerating the significance of adverse events and trivialize the importance of positive events. These are unconscious happenings that maintain the main negative schema of a depressed person even while there is contrary evidence. As a result, they feel hopeless, about themselves, and the future disregarding evidence and opinion that things can improve.

In Conclusion

This chapter has laid a foundation for depression. Without a doubt, there are many treatment options for depression, including medication. However, that is not the focus of this chapter. The next chapter will shed light on how CBT techniques can help manage and eventually get rid of depression.

Chapter 6:
CBT the Unique Depression Cure

CBT can be used as a talk therapy which is more effective than medication for some people in addressing depression. It can handle mild, moderate, and severe cases of depression with a very skilled therapist, and by yourself, if you have the right knowledge.

Cognitive Behavioral Therapy for Depression Technique

In using CBT to get rid of depression, the first goal is to reduce depression through cognitive and behavioral techniques. With this, the client can identify and challenge irrational thoughts. After a notable improvement in the condition, these individuals can then practice a schema-focused approach to guard against relapse. The goal of this phase is to recognize and replace dysfunctional schemas which trigger depressive episodes

Behavioral Strategies

This is usually the first stage when using CBT to cure depression. One common characteristic of people with depression is a significant reduction in activity levels. This explains why many people with depression will lock themselves up in the room and play a video game rather than go to work, attend a social gathering like a dinner party, etc. This be a repetitive cycle in which horrible life events triggers depression and other sour emotional responses which causes withdrawal and avoidance behavior. This leads to a vicious cycle that tends to reinforce the depressive symptoms.

Behavioral strategies are employed to combat this and reduce avoidance. We also use it to increase the patients' involvement in activities (activities that bring pleasure and fulfillment) that will reduce depressive symptoms. Hence, the aim of this will be to replace avoidance tendencies with activation behaviors which break the vicious cycle of depression and improve the mood.

A graded approach is usually used in assigning activities which typically start with less complex ones and gradually graduates to difficult ones. This happens through the course of the treatment as the patient becomes more responsive. A patient, for instance with mild to moderate depression, could be initially asked to go to a cinema (pleasurable activity) and dedicate about 10 minutes to work (accomplishment). The overall aim is to engage the patient at their current depressive level and gradually engage them with activities.

For activity scheduling to be effective, you will need an activity rating form, since you are working on yourself. With this, patients keep track of their activities during the day and give a rating of how each activity brought a sense of accomplishment and mastery.

Completed Daily Activity Monitoring Sheet

This is useful data to challenge the patient's belief that they can't enjoy or be fulfilled from any activities again. It is also a valuable tool for the therapist to know the kind of activity they can assign as homework in the future which could trigger the feeling of pleasure, fulfillment, and mastery. For assigned activities to be completed successfully, you will have to engage in cognitive or imaginary rehearsal. This involves the patient visualizing themselves participating in different activities for them to detect anything that can prevent them from enjoying or having a sense of fulfillment with the events. With these, you can focus on solving these embargos which leads to an increased chance of gaining achievement with the assigned activity.

There could also be extra behavioral strategies to help with other problems that trigger the depressive symptoms of the patient. For a patient with an abnormal eating disorder, they could be open to ways to bring their eating pattern under control. In the same manner, patients having issues with social skills will need extra treatment that addresses specific skill defects. This will improve their ability to complete the scheduled assignment and gain the expected fulfillment from such activities. To improve social deficit, for instance, you might use assertive training, social skill training, and other exercises that target social and communication skills.

Initial Cognitive Strategies

With this, the aim is to extract common automatic thoughts that have affected you and are responsible for the depressive episodes. They will further test these thoughts and bring out the core schemas that affect the patient's view of the world. Automatic thoughts are mental images or activities which spring up in response to a trigger (an event or action).

Automatic thoughts are usually frequent, not often noticed by the individual; hence they are generally accepted as truths and facts without examination. People with depression have these automatic thoughts which are harmful and correspond to the cognitive triads which keep them deep down the hole of depression. Some typical examples of automatic thoughts which trigger depression are thoughts like: "I can never get anything done right," "I am such a failure," "no one likes me."

The first step often is recognizing and bringing to notice these automatic thoughts. A standard method employed by CBT therapists is to ask questions that relate to those thoughts that spring up in response to different events. The therapist can also use role-playing to recreate past events to examine various ideas that the patient has in the process, which you can also apply on your own. During the process of recognizing automatic thoughts, it is also essential for the patient to take note of the mood changes that occur as the automatic thoughts spring up. This will help them learn and understand the influence that these thoughts have on their emotions. For this step to be useful, you will have to keep a journal of your feelings alongside the automatic thoughts that arise as a result of the distressing situations that happen, even in the therapy sessions.

After identifying these automatic thoughts, the next step often is for you to challenge these negative automatic thoughts. You will have to write down other columns in the thought record journal. These would include columns that shed light on the distressing events, shedding light on emotions alongside the negative automatic thoughts, prescribe a different and sensible reaction to the events, and express the feelings that come with their new belief system.

These detailed records can be specific to each person to help challenge the unique cognitive distortion particular to the patient. However, the main aim is to consider evidence that supports or challenges these negative automatic thoughts and replace them with something rational and realistic which will hardly lead to depression.

Cognitive Distortions

To challenge an automatic negative thought such as "I am a failure," the therapist might ask further questions like "how do you know you are a failure?". This time, you will have to ask and answer the question on your own. There will be following questions that will examine each piece of evidence to ascertain whether the evidence proves the belief that the person is a failure. Over time, it has been discovered that individuals with depression do not have adequate evidence to bolster the belief they so much hold on to. They, however, give the wrong interpretation to available cues so that it keeps them in a depressed state for longer.

You can also complete a behavioral test to examine negative thoughts. For this to be effective, however, you must agree that such thoughts can be monitored and altered. There are times that the patients might not be in such agreement. This is where the CBT therapist will introduce an additional discussion on the patient's maladaptive thoughts and symptoms of depression. After agreeing to test the negative thinking concerning reality, the patient must also decide to go through a behavioral test.

With the behavioral test, the patient would keep track of how the behavior went as well as its relation to negative thoughts and come to some conclusions. The patient, with the therapist, will also want to review the findings which are kept on the thought record. An example of a behavioral test with a patient dealing with the negative thought "no one likes me" is to try and get him or her to spend time with others. The therapist could ask them to call five specific individuals and ask for a get together anytime in the future. Along with the therapist, they discuss what the patient will say while making the call and other aspects to ensure the endeavor is successful. The next section will be to review the results and analyze how the results contradict or support the assertion that no one likes the patient!

Altering Maladaptive Schemas

As soon as the patient has benefited from the first stage of the treatment with a sign of significant improvement in their depressive symptoms, the treatment approach can change. With CBT, the therapist (or patient in this case) can focus on preventing relapse by trying to change core schemas.

Compared to negative thoughts, schemas are tricky to change as they are believed to arise from past events that occurred in early life. This phase relates more to the pattern of development, interpersonal relationships (as well as a patient-therapist relationship), and emotional experience.

This phase will begin by delving and assessing your history, with the intention to identify potential schemas. It doesn't stop at this; the therapist will ensure that the patient is well informed about the effect and influence of schemas and people. After the completion of this preliminary change, the next step is to try and change such maladaptive schemas.

The strategies employed in this are pretty much like the steps introduced in the first stage of treatment like scheduling, cognitive restructuring, etc. However, the focus of this is on a longstanding pattern which repeats situations in a strategic way because of the maladapted schemas.

Cognitive Behavioral Therapy for Major Depression

You can also decide to use Albert Ellis' techniques to take care of depression. With this technique, you can understand the series of events that causes depression. This usually happens in steps which, and for the ease of remembering, are generally identified by A, B, C, D, and E – the first five letters of the alphabet. According to Ellis:

A refers to Activating experiences like relationship stress, memories of past traumas, dissatisfaction with work, a failed romantic date, and any event could trigger an immediate sadness in the person.

B refers to false and irrational Beliefs which trigger sadness; for instance, no one likes me, I am a failure at everything I do, and I can never get anything done right, etc.

C refers to the Consequence of such beliefs which manifests as symptoms of depression and negative emotions that arise from false thinking.

While the process of activating or recalling traumatic experience could be painful, it should be emphasized that the feelings and emotions from these experiences create the reaction (symptoms of depression). Thus, past traumatic experience has no hold on you; instead, your emotional response to such experience is the source of the problem. This leads us to the fourth alphabet where:

The cognitive therapist teaches the patient how to Dispute these false beliefs. With these, you can develop positive psychological effects of rational thinking.

This usually forms the basis of using Cognitive Behavioral Therapy to help patients with depression. The premise of using Cognitive Behavioral Therapy to tackle depression is to recognize their irrational thoughts and correct them with facts. The correction process will involve helping the patient see reasons with a set of systematic questions why their irrational thoughts have no basis. The following example illustrates how CBT helps disprove irrational thoughts

The patient will reveal one of the automatic negative thoughts to the cognitive therapist; for instance, "I am good at nothing." The cognitive therapist will help examine how true this thought is by asking if it is true that she is good at nothing. The therapist might ask for a list of things she has done and failed woefully at, as well as things she has done well. For instance, the decision to take up CBT for improvement points to the fact that she wants to get help; she is after her wellbeing. Hence, she is good at something! With this, the therapist can help the patient conclude that such thinking pattern is entirely untrue and not to be taken seriously.

One of the aims of CBT is that after multiple sessions, the client can pay attention to their thoughts and challenge them on their own! This helps prevent relapse!

Retraining Your Brain with Cognitive Behavioral Therapy

To the behavioral aspect of CBT, the focus here will be suggesting healthy coping behaviors to the patient, as a replacement to other ones. With the help of a CBT therapist, the patient can pass an expression as problematic or not, as well as a skill deficit. The therapist also presents other healthy appropriate behaviors, as well as education on missing skill sets. For instance, mindfulness, meditation, going for a walk, breathing techniques, and other forms of activities, could help cope with depression. Hence, for a patient that has withdrawn socially, CBT recommends exercise or other forms of socialization. A role-playing technique which involves engaging in new behaviors and different types of activities are techniques that CBT does recommend helping the patient get better.

We have emphasized the importance of homework during CBT sessions. This is effective during the therapy which involves keeping a journal of thoughts, behaviors, and mood, including their efforts towards combating such irrational thoughts and other cognitive restructuring exercises. We also recommend clients to keep tabs of improvements they see as they adopt new thinking habits. Once they are fully aware of the negative pattern in their thought process and moods, they can also try out new skills with the help of their journal and compare the improvements they see.

Aside from combating and disputing negative thoughts and behaviors, a therapist can also teach patients how to break complicated and overwhelming tasks into smaller and manageable components. This increases the chances of achieving success with such activities. CBT can help depressed people get rid of the fear of facing an overwhelming task which could help reduce anxiety and avoidance. This helps improve mood, boost confidence, and makes them feel good about themselves.

Chapter 7:
The Anxiety, Fear, Worry, Phobia Triggers

Anxiety: Symptoms and Triggers
Stress is a reasonable emotion built into humans by nature. However, when anxiety and stress levels get out of hand, it can be a mental disorder. It is a class of mental health illness that triggers excessive nervousness, worry, and fear.

Anxiety disorder does affect how one responds to an event and their resulting behavior which manifests in physical symptoms. While pure anxiety might not be a cause for concern, severe anxiety might affect daily living.

What Is Anxiety?
Anxiety can be said to be an unreasonable reaction to tensions. According to the American Psychological Association (APA), anxiety is:

"An emotion characterized by feelings of tension, worried thoughts and physical changes like increased blood pressure."(American Psychological Association)

In the face of danger, anxiety is normal for survival. Since the time of our forefathers, the slightest sign of danger triggers some form of alarm in the body which prepares the body for survival action. These alarms manifest in the form of an increased heartbeat, sweating, etc.

This event triggers a rush of adrenalin, a chemical messenger and hormone in the brain. This leads to the body's anxious reaction, also called the "fight-or-flight" response. With this, a man can either confront or flee from a potential threat.

There are times when the body's response to the anxious feeling can be disproportionate to the trigger. This could manifest in the form of nausea or increased blood pressure. This has graduated from normal anxiety to anxiety disorder. Anxiety now revolves around relationships, health, work, money, and other life areas, when there is no real threat to life.

According to the American Psychological Association (APA), anxiety disorder is:

"having recurring intrusive thoughts or concerns."

Once anxiety graduates to this stage, typical day to day activities will be impaired.

Signs of Anxiety

Many things can point out to anxiety in humans. Some of these are:

- A feeling of restlessness
- A helpless feeling of worry
- Difficulty in concentration
- Excessive irritability
- Problem falling and staying asleep
- Digestive issues
- Weakness and dizziness
- Fatigue
- Shaking and sweating
- Rapid heart rate
- Panic attack in severe cases

Causes and Risk Factor of Anxiety

While the medical field has no definite reason for anxiety, some factors encourage its onset.

Environmental Stressors like work issues, relationship problems, and problems in the family.

It could also be genetic. People who have family members with a history of anxiety disorder are more likely to experience it.

It could also be medical and manifest as the symptom of a disease, or the effect of a medication, or the stress from a long recovery.

Faulty brain wiring as psychologists revealed that uneven hormones and signals could trigger anxiety in the brain.

It could also manifest as a withdrawal symptom from illicit substances.

Fear: Symptoms and Causes

Emotion is critical in the day to day living of humans. One such emotion is fear, which is programmed into man and animal as a natural response to any form of threat. Biologically speaking, when someone experiences fear, some part of the brain is activated (like the amygdala and the hypothalamus.)

Fear is not always adaptive. A small dose of fear before giving a presentation is healthy and will serve a purpose – to make you give your best to the presentation. This is one of the types of 'useful fear.' Fear could, however, be excessive and damaging which could make you want to escape when it is not reasonable.

There are times general fear or fear of something gets out of control. This can get to the point where regular and daily activities become impaired. Fear is neither adaptive nor reasonable when we dread events that haven't happened yet.

Fear and uncertainty of the future are called anxiety. Fear occurs the moment danger arises while anxiety arises because we do not know what is going to happen next. When we experience fear, some chemicals like cortisol (stress hormone) and adrenaline get into the blood. This manifests in the form of:

- Muscle tightening
- Pupil dilation
- Excessive sweating
- Increased blood pressure
- Excessive heart rate

People subjected to fear know the exact time that the danger arose and how time seemed to crawl. Without any effort, they knew what to do and how they felt so powerful to overcome the threat that confronted them.

Causes of Fear

It is critically important to be aware of potential threats. However, it is more important to react to them the right way. For many people, the proper response is to experience a calming of the initial reaction as soon as the sign of danger is past.

This is, however, not the case for some people. Fear has become maladaptive for many people as they struggle with panic attacks, anxiety, and phobia – extreme forms of fear. Children are also at more significant risk since they are not developed enough to rationalize fear as unrealistic.

Fear is complex. Some could be due to trauma while others could be an indication of fear of something definite, such as a loss of a job. There is also fear that could be due to physical symptoms; for instance, fear of water makes you want to pass out.

Phobia: Symptoms and Causes
Phobia is defined as an irrational or unreasonable fear of an object or situation. It is a pretty common form of anxiety disorder which makes people avoid the object or condition. This is a prevalent form of a mental illness which can have a minor or severe effect on the victim.

A person with a phobia might avoid the trigger such as rat or snake or situations like crowds or heights. People with a severe phobia will do all in their power to avoid the source of their fear. This can affect the victim's ability to function normally in society, or in the presence of the object they dread.

Several theories exist regarding the cause of phobias, although there is no specific cause identified. Although, the cause of phobia varies depending on the phobia type. However, phobia could be associated with a frightening event, stressful experience, or even a family member with a phobia that got passed on to a child, etc.

Symptoms of Phobias

These symptoms of phobia are peculiar to the various forms of phobia. The signs are:

- An excessive form of anxiety when confronted with the source of fear

- A compulsive avoidance of the origin of fear

- Paralysis or distorted function on exposure to the trigger

One thing about folks with a phobia is that they acknowledge that the fear does not make sense and it's often exaggerated. This is usually accompanied by a feeling of helplessness. These manifest in some physical effects like abnormal breathing pattern, chills, sweating, chest pain or tightness, trembling, a choking sensation, nausea, dizziness, etc.

Thinking about the source of the trigger could also trigger anxiety in the victim. Parents might observe this in their kids. This could manifest as excessive crying, being clingy, hiding between their legs or under the table, etc.

Worry: Causes and Symptoms

Worry is an excessive feeling or concern about a situation in which we have no control. Worrying causes the mind to replay what might happen in the future which causes the body to overdrive.

Excessive worry might trigger anxiety and sometimes panic. Many people with severe worrying tendencies do have a feeling of an impending great calamity which increases their fear and buttresses their worry.

Excessive worrying might negatively affect a person's day to day activity. It could adversely reduce your performance at work, interfere with sleep, relationship, and job, etc. People prone to excessive worrying are also susceptible to anxiety and they resort to dangerous habits and lifestyles, such as alcohol, cigarette smoking and overeating as a coping mechanism.

Worry can manifest itself as restlessness, uneasiness, lack of sleep, difficulty with concentration, etc. The next section discusses how CBT helps with these.

How CBT Helps with Anxiety, Worry, And Fear

People survive in environments that meet their needs. This explains why the kind of environment a person is in can guard against addiction and help fulfillment. Humans have innate needs, as well as an inherent desire to meet them. We end up suffering when we cannot meet these needs.

Happiness is not a result of what you do. It involves identifying actions to meet your needs. This explains why people who meet their needs will be less likely to suffer anxiety or fear. The same way hunger tells you that you are not meeting a need, fear and anxiety is a signal to a need you are not meeting. Some CBT techniques to help with anxiety and fear are:

Concentrate on How Feelings Change

Bear in mind that feelings do change. Hence, whenever you are confronted with a feeling of anxiety, worry, or fear direct your thoughts to how better you will feel once the feeling changes. It is always recommended to write those thoughts down.

Hence, to a person who is anxious about a thesis defense, he might write something like,

"I am bombarded with nervousness which is quite expected. I do expect to feel peace and relaxed when this feeling changes and clear my head."

In addition to the feeling, it also helps to note the physical changes that come with a change of feeling. For a person preparing for a thesis defense, for instance, he would be able to pass across his argument in a clear and concise manner. This is worth jotting down as well.

Consider It and Act Normal

Anxiety and fear are a normal survival response and not an illness; it, however, is a response that can be damaging at times. Just like when your security dog bites the leg of the pizza man thinking it is helping, your anxiety response gets the best of you thinking it's helping, even though the threat might be unreal. However, by giving feedback and being "picky" with what you allow, you can get ahold of anxiety and fear.

Fear and anxiety are fed from what the victim does alongside emotional pattern matching. This explains why anxiety and fear will disappear if the victim acts as if they are not in a critical situation. For instance, you will hardy smile, talk softly, take a deep breath, or go into an open body posture in an emergency period.

Adopting any of the behaviors above, even one, when we feel anxious disturbs the regular feedback to the fear response system. Our sympathetic nervous system interprets this as since he is smiling, salivating, talking normally, chewing gum then there is no real threat.

No one will ever think of eating in a stressful situation or life-threatening situation that trigger fear. Hence, if people act normal and even chew gum in the face of a threat, it can alter the feedback loop and close anxiety, which is the idea, to trick the anxiety feedback system and disturb its flow.

Anxiety, fear, and worry are all about expectation which could be disastrous. With this, we move to the next technique.

Stop the basic Assumption and Analyze the Logical Conclusion.

Someone who is fearful, worried, or anxious about something; dreads some form of consequence. However, what is the consequence?

If I fear public speaking, for instance, I should ask myself: "What consequence do I fear?"

I might assume: "I fear making a fool of myself."

What will be the consequence? They will not like me.

And the consequence of that: I will be sad.

And the consequence of that: I will feel I am good for nothing.

This can go on for so long. However, how do we deal with this?

You will remember all those that did not like you.

With time, the memory of the failed attempt at public speaking will fade.

Then, I realize how wrong I can be when I assume people do not like me.

When people do this, they see that the consequence is not some disastrous end but a phase which they could correct.

Exposure In CBT: Facing Fear

Ideally, people will do all in their capacity to stay away from what causes anxiety in them. This explains why someone with a phobia will avoid the trigger like the plague. However, the issue with staying away from the trigger is that it robs you of learning that what you fear is not as dangerous as you think it is. In this case, a person with agoraphobia who completely avoids all social gatherings will not be able to learn that not all social gatherings are a threat to survival.

CBT terms the process of facing one's fear as exposure. It is the most vital step in learning to manage anxiety and fear effectively. With publicity, you are gradually introduced to the source of thing you dread till the anxiety reduces. The exposure, however, must be gradual till you can confidently deal with things that make your anxiety level go haywire.

The first usually involves writing down things, experiences and situations you fear. A person with agoraphobia, for instance, will avoid public places at all cost. Such a person will have a list that includes: the mall, the park, the football field, the theater, a rally or a stadium. He could, however, start gradually by taking a walk on his street for a week before graduating to going to the park. He could do this with a therapist or a friend. On having a list, start from the least scary event and gradually graduate with time.

Once you can take a walk down your street with less anxiety, you can graduate to the next scary event. In CBT this technique for managing phobia, fear, and anxiety is essential to face fears daily. With intense practice, you can feel your phobia and anxiety disappearing. This leads to positive progress as you continue in your bid to improve.

Chapter 8:
Daily CBT Exercise for Anxiety, Fear, Worry, Phobia

The Importance of Cognitive Behavioral Therapy Exercise

We have seen throughout the preceding chapters how CBT helps people with a mental issue by presenting a reasonable approach of coming to terms with difficult situations. Cognitive Behavioral Therapy teaches that when people have a psychological problem, it usually involves thoughts, behaviors, and emotions. Hence, when we analyze challenging situations in the light of these three, getting a form of solution and intervention is easy.

This explains why people constantly bombarded with negative thoughts will have a resulting chain reaction of negative emotions and behavior. Hence, in helping people like this, examining and reconfiguring the thought is the best way. Should the negative thinking trigger a wrong behavioral pattern, learning a new behavior as a replacement is usually a good response.

Many times, these three essential components (thoughts, behaviors, and emotions) are usually connected to mental issues. With Cognitive Behavioral Therapy exercise, you can examine each of the components.

For a person with a phobia, for instance, CBT exercises can help such person identify the fault in his / her thinking pattern. This will reduce the intensity of the anxiety when the patient can realize that it's all in his / her head.

CBT Exercise for Anxiety

Many people are faced with anxiety which happens due to a faulty idea of reality and future events. This set of people could obsess with something and imagine all sort of worse scenarios. This manifests in physical and sometimes emotional forms that affect the life and regular daily activity of the person.

Anxiety mainly is the result of distorted expectation. This is what CBT aims to counter. With CBT exercise, the patient can learn to replace these thoughts with ones that accurately depict reality. It is also a way to build confidence since negative and unrealistic expectations about oneself are challenged and altered.

When you challenge and change negative thought about yourself, your ability, and the future it does have a positive effect on your emotions. With this, the next section discusses some helpful CBT techniques to fight anxiety disorder.

Cognitive Restructuring

The basics of cognitive restructuring involve challenging thought and accessing it using reality as a judge. Let us examine the case of a lady preparing for an interview. Despite optimum preparation on her part, she still cannot shake off the feeling of anxiety. To help ease this anxious feeling, she had to keep a diary over the week to keep track of her negative thoughts. Often, a common thought that she has is "I am going to screw up the interview," despite various preparation for the interview. On the next visit to her CBT therapist, she discusses this thought and the therapist asks why she thinks she will screw up her interview. She responds: my heart races and I feel like I am being interrogated.

Sam's therapist explains that worry and anxiety are responsible for her unsettled mind. The excessive worry could also affect her optimum performance which could make her feel underprepared no matter how prepared she is. Sam, in the strength of this confidence, counters the thought and changes it to. "I am only anxious; I am well prepared to handle all questions at this interview."

This is the basis of cognitive restructuring – switching negative thoughts or expectations to pretty positive ones. One must be willing to identify these negative thoughts, question them with facts and change them to positive and encouraging ones, even without a therapist, the premise is the same.

Behavioral Exercise

Sam, still in the process of preparing for her interview, keeps her diary. With time, she, however, learned to switch her thoughts to positive ones and keeps tabs on this process and its effect on her anxiety levels. This is the process of conducting a behavioral experiment which requires trial and error and is a task for the patient. This can help get to the primary cause of the negative thought that triggers anxiety.

Recording and Challenging Faulty Thought Patterns

It does not only stop at collecting negative thoughts. Sam does have a list of negative thoughts and perception as they pop up. The CBT therapist informed Sam to gather evidence for or against the thought. For instance, when she thinks: "Even if I am hired, I do not have enough skill to perform well." The next task is to gather evidence for or against this thought. Her journal looks like the table below:

Evidence in Support of Tom's Thought

- I have no experience since I have not done this before

Evidence Against Tom's Thought

- I graduated with good grades

- I will learn on the job

- Adequate training facilities

- I am diligent at what I do

- I will have a mentor to look up to

From the table above, it is glaring that the evidence against Sam's deluded thought of not performing up to expectation is much more than the evidence in support. This alone is a boost that can give Sam superb confidence, ready to resume with bright hope and anticipation of her dazzling performance at her new job post.

With this type of CBT technique for anxiety, one can combat anxiety.

Daily CBT Exercise for Phobia

A person is said to have a phobia when he or she has an unrealistic fear of an event, a place, or an animal. Phobia manifests itself in the form of anxiety as a response to the feared object. The anxiety is usually so intense that it affects normal functioning. Phobia can be treated, and CBT has proven very helpful to handle phobia.

Many people, with just a short course of CBT, do show tremendous improvement when treating phobia with CBT. The basic approach of CBT involved dissociating the severe anxiety response from the feared object. This happens through the identification of the irrational thinking pattern. This is followed by a new, adaptive way of thinking. As soon as these thought patterns become familiar and proven realistic, CBT will suggest helpful behavioral adaptations where they get to face their fear which wouldn't trigger anxiety.

Because phobia differs from person to person, CBT technique to combat it varies. However, the treatment plan falls under the following:

Cognitive Restructuring

Phobia often manifests as devastating and catastrophic thoughts that often paralyzes the victim. Besides, people with a phobia do feel helpless in the face of the object or situation of dread. They are entirely unaware of their ability to keep calm in such a situation. With Cognitive Behavioral Therapy exercise, such people can identify such horrible thoughts and swap them with pretty realistic ones which reduce the anxiety response.

Systematic Exposure

With regular exposure, people find a way to confront what they dread. It happens continually until they get to the point where it triggers little or no anxiety. This is a step by step approach in which the patient starts with the anxiety-provoking stimulus. On getting comfortable with the first stimuli, the person can expose himself to a pretty intense stimulus and try to get comfortable with it.

The case of a person with dentophobia, for instance, could begin by discussing with a friend who has had a dental treatment before about the process. On getting comfortable with this, he could even watch YouTube videos about the dental process. When he feels prepared, he can take a trip, alongside the therapist or a loved one to the dental clinic and will realize that a dental procedure will not kill him nor cause severe pain as the imagination has made him believe.

For exposure to work best, however, there must be cognitive restructuring as the foundation. This is because there must be a change in thinking pattern for patterns of anxiety to decrease when people are faced with their fear.

Mindfulness Training

With mindfulness, you bring your thought and attention to reality and what is happening at present. This is a vital part of phobia treatment because when faced with the fear scenario, it is usually the thought that paralyzes them with anxiety and panic, not the feared object or situation. Many people get so lost in the thoughts of woe or bad scenario that they zone out. And yet, most times, the feared object means no harm. In other words, they get so carried away by the mental visualization going on in their head that the harmless environment means nothing to them.

Hence, when confronted with the source of phobia the next time, try deep breathing and focusing your attention on the breath. This will bring your attention to the present and serve to calm your nerves.

CBT Exercise for Worry: Worry Script

When we talk about worry, most of the time, it involves situations in which one has little or no control. Hence, a useful tool to deal with excessive worry is worry script. Most times, people worry about things like:

- Being able to meet the expectation of spouse and work

- The safety of your family, friends, and loved ones

- Worry about what the future holds.

When we worry, we waste time and energy which triggers a massive dose of anxiety. As it has been discussed in previous sections, the best way to face fear is gradual exposure to the source of fear. However, herein lies the problem: You can use continuous exposure to get rid of your fear of spiders. This is practically useless when it relates to fear of what is yet to happen.

Since continuous exposure will not help here, we recommend what is called the worry script. This is just like a journal or daily script where you write down your worst fear for a week or two.

The Usefulness of a Worry Script

One of the common traits peculiar to people with generalized anxiety disorder is the inability to put their negative emotions (sadness or fear) in check. They are used to adopting techniques that don't help with their condition – either pushing away the feelings or trying to think about something else.

Here is the problem with this approach:

One flaw with trying to push bad thoughts away is that it doesn't work. If you have ever wanted to do it, you will acknowledge how easy it is for such evil thoughts to come back. This is not surprising as it takes a lot of work to keep bad thoughts away.

Some people, on the other hand, are fond of switching from one worry topic to another. They, in their bid to keep their anxiety down switch from one worry topic to the other. This approach is faulty because it robs you of the opportunity of getting to understand your fear. Instead, you resort to dodging upsetting feelings by replacing your worries.

Worry script is different in that it brings you face to face with your fear, not literally this time around. Hence, rather than channeling your energy on dodging upsetting thoughts and mental images, it is a good idea to face your fears. Write down the negative thoughts as they pop in your head as worry. This will allow you to understand what you are worked up about, as well as a chance to come to terms with your anxiety. This way, you change your emotional response to the source of worry.

Many people have attempted a worry script and reported how they felt less anxious about the issues they write down.

While a typical man tends to worry about a lot of situations, the good news is that they do fit into one or two categories. In other words, many things people worry about might be grouped under an idea.

For instance, worries about being a lousy parent, losing your job, underperforming at your workplace all fall under the category of personal failure (It must do more of general life success). With a worry script, issues you worry about under a similar category will reduce.

How to Write A Worry Script?

For your worry script to be ideal, it should be the worst-case scenario for one of the things you worry about. For instance, you could have a worry script about failed parenting.

Your script should be as detailed as possible.

In other words, explore all your senses in writing down the script. Write what you feel will happen, tap into your imagination and be brutal. Worry script about failed parenting for instance, you might describe your son doing drugs, being mischievous to the neighbors, joining one of the worst gangs or cults in the history of man, being dragged in by the law enforcement, your visit to him in prison, your son in the orange prison clothes.

Bear in mind that it is perfect to be anxious and upset during the process. This is good since your worry script is supposed to be about your worst-case scenario; hence, being upset is fine.

Besides, the worry script aims to give a permanent solution to your worries and anxiety. Hence, be prepared to bear the pain of facing your fears and worst-case scenarios while having this exercise.

Since this is a daily exercise, schedule a time to make entries into your worry script daily. Devote yourself to it and avoid distractions.

Let every day be a gift in which you get to tackle every bit of worry. Devote every day to encounter a new worry and explore it deeper as you write your script. For instance, a script could be about how disappointing your spouse could be deadly to your relationship.

With time, as you devote yourself to writing the worry script, you will discover that the anxiety fades and you do not feel worked up about this issue. It is not a magic process as it will take time, weeks before you notice any tangible changes.

Chapter 9:
Identify what Unleashes the Hulk

Reflect on your previous week and think about what made you angry. You might have things like:

- Your kids not following instructions

- Your opinion that was disregarded at the workplace

- The mailman misplacing your mail

- The driver before you are driving too slowly

- The bank that sends you a reminder of a loan you already cleared etc.

What makes people angry differs and the list could be endless. However, the in-exhaustive list of what makes people angry can be grouped into three:

- Failure to meet our goals and expectations

- When we feel threatened or cheated

- An attempt to hide emotions (a common habit of men when they try to cover up feelings of fear or sadness)

These three factors account for all causes of anger. In trying to understand the anger, knowledge of these three is critical.

The Thinking Pattern of An Angry Man

The very first response of the body to anger is switching to the fight or flight mode. If you are the confrontational type, you go to the fight mode. You raise your voice, display aggression, accuse people, and defend yourself with a vivid display of negative body language. While these behaviors are harmful, the emotions of anger suppress our ability to interpret these actions as dangerous.

On the other hand, the non-confrontational type will withdraw and switch to the flight mode. He will walk out on his spouse at the heat of an argument or run to the restroom if at the office. This is the instinct directing him to flee. This is also unhelpful as you are left with bottled up emotions which could sour your mood and make you aggressive toward others and even irritable.

Everyone gets angry. However, the level or intensity of the anger differs. For people who can control their anger, there is no lasting effect. People who get angry quickly and become aggressive could be prone to serious health consequences.

Consider a time you were angry, and you probably had an increase in your heart rate which made your blood pressure rise. If this happens continuously, there is a high risk of cardiovascular issues, especially with the heart.

Besides your health, anger is damaging to the people and relationships around you. No matter how you think your anger is justified, or the urge to react, the consequence of anger is devastating as it impairs judgment, affects success, and tarnishes your image.

This is where anger management comes in.

Anger Management and Its Goal

Anger management is much more than trying to suppress anger because trying to do so is not healthy. Anger is an entirely normal emotion which is part of the DNA wiring of all humans. Hence, no matter how hard you try to suppress anger, it will erupt. With anger management, however, you can learn to decode the signals coming from your emotions, get them in control and healthily express them. With this, you will have a strong relationship with people, and you will appear responsible as well.

Anger management is not a straightforward task. With practice, however, you can get the grasp of it. With anger management, you can manage your life well since you can put the emotions in check.

How to Put Your Anger in Check?

Find Out Why You Are Angry

Anger issues and the emotions that accompany it usually come from things you learned as a child. Hence, a child that grew up watching people yell at each other, throw things, etc. will think that it is the right way to express anger. Besides, excessive stress and past events could make you prone to anger.

Most times, anger is usually an expression of something else.

Therefore, you do need to know what is upsetting you, for you to express yourself well. Anger, often, is known to mask other feelings like shame, embarrassment, vulnerability, or shame. This explains why a man that cannot provide for his family could become suddenly angry or irritable.

With this, if your default response to a series of things life throws at you is anger, then getting in touch with your real feeling might be hard. This is prevalent in families where they hardly express their feelings. Kids in this household will grow up and get angry easily, rather than expressing their feelings. It should also be pointed out that anger could be one of the underlying symptoms of mental health issues like chronic stress and depression.

CLUES TO KNOW YOUR ANGER IS COVERING UP OTHER FEELINGS
You Think Expressing Other Emotions Makes You Vulnerable

In other words, you like it when people think you are tough and in control. You feel that you are not capable of emotions like guilt, shame, or fear that make you weak and don't apply to you. The flaw in this mentality is that everyone is wired with these emotions and your inability to display them is revealed via anger.

You Hardly Compromise
These are the type of people that fail to reason with others. They rarely see things from other people's point of view. People who grew up in a family with anger issues will notice that most of the household got their way by being loud and aggressive. You feel like a failure when you compromise.

Different Opinion Is A Challenge
In other words, you are always right and angry with people who disagree with your view. You also have this inherent need to be in control. Therefore, you don't accommodate other people's way of thinking as it is a challenge to your authority. You don't take challenges lightly and you must argue even to your last breath to prove a point.

If you are confronted with various emotions and you find it difficult to compromise, the next step is to try and get in touch with your feelings. By reconnecting with your feelings, you can better manage anger rather than cover it up with other emotions

Know What Triggers Your Anger and The Warning Signs

Retraining Your Brain with Cognitive Behavioral Therapy

You do not just explode into anger suddenly, there are subtle physical warning signs in your body. Anger is one of the many normal emotions programmed into a person. Anger activates the "fight or flight" hormone in the body; the intensity of these hormones depends on how angry you are. However, when you know the signs your body gives when you are about to lose it, you can take steps to control yourself.

Take note of how your body feels and keep tabs on the thoughts that get you angry.

Many people have concluded that anger is a result of external events – For instance, the actions of insensitive people and situations beyond your control. However, anger is related to what you feel about what happened and how you interpreted it, rather than what happened. Some faulty thinking patterns that fuel anger are:

Over-generalization: You ALWAYS leave the door open. You NEVER do what I ask of you. EVERYONE sees me as a failure.

Collecting Straws: Intentionally focusing on things that get on your nerves while you ignore past positive ones.

Blaming: In other words, every other person is responsible for things that went wrong and didn't go according to plan

Stay Away from People, Things, And Situations That Make You Boil

That you are stressed is not an excuse for anger. Instead, we recommend that you get to know the effects of these events on you and your environment. This will allow you to take charge of your environment and keep aggravations in check. Examine your daily routines and discover situations, activities, places, and people that unleash the hulk. You might get angry every time the mailman misplaces your mail. Give the situation another approach such that it doesn't get you worked up.

Identify Ways to Calm Down

In addition to knowing the signs that the hulk in you is rising as well as what unleashes it, the next step is to learn ways to promptly tame the hulk before it gets out of control. There are many ways you can cool down and keep anger in check.

Some of these are:

- Take deep breaths: when you breathe slowly and deeply, it can weaken tension build up. The idea is to get more fresh air into your lungs.

- Walking Away: Taking a walk to the restroom or around the block is a good idea. You can approach the situation from a better perspective since negative energy is released.

- Employ Your Senses: There is relaxation in engaging any of the five senses. Hence, you might choose to listen to music or go for your favorite snack.

- Take another Approach: When someone says something meant to get on your nerves; for instance, the typical response will be to yell at the person and get mad. However, talk calmly and probably smile. This disrupts any sensation of anger that might build up in your body.

- The next time you are about to get angry, have a reality check and take a moment to ruminate over the situation. Your feedback could alter your approach.

Employ Healthy Coping Mechanisms

There are times when anger could be the only response mechanism. However, the difference here is that you can choose to express yourself in a healthy manner. When anger is channeled responsibly, the effect can be amazing.

Know Exactly What Is Upsetting

Many couples, for instance, fight and argue over silly and minute things. If not careful, it could escalate into a big fight. For example, not taking out the trash or the dishes left undone. However, often, there is more to the anger. Hence, take time to know what you are angry about when you find your irritations building up. When you know what is getting you all worked up, you can take a constructive step to communicate your anger well.

Pause When Things Heat Up

When you feel the hulk in you misbehaving, take a step back and get away from the situation for a couple of minutes or as long as you think you need. A walk down the beach, or to the park, a few moments of enjoying your favorite music could help release tension. This gives you a clear head to approach the matter.

Always Fight Fair
The danger of not fighting fair is the breakdown of the relationship and other irreparable damage that might come as a result of the anger. When you fight fair, however, you see things from the other's angle while also expressing yourself.

Choose Your Battles
Conflicts and anger release negative energy which could be draining. Hence, take a step back every time you are about to get angry and decide if the issue is worth getting worked up over. Besides, choosing the issues to fight about makes people take you seriously when upset, compared to someone who makes a fuss over every little thing.

Know When to Let Go
There are times you might not be able to come to an agreement with others. Be wise enough to know that the conflict is not going anywhere and disengage. Preserving a relationship is better than winning a battle.

Work on Your Conflict Resolution Skills
Conflict and disagreement themselves are damaging. However, your mode of approach also determines whether there will be hostility, or

you get to build safety and trust. The positive resolution of the conflict will go a long way to keep anger in check and preserve relationships.

Seek Professional Help

Anger has so much gotten the best of some people that every control tactic they learned disappears in the heat of the anger. Some cases in which getting professional help will be ideal are:

- You cannot seem to shake off the feeling of anger and frustration

- Your temper is already interfering with your work and relationship

- You avoid meeting people because you feel you might lose it

- The law enforcement agency has arrested you before due to anger

- The tendency to be physically violent when angry

Introducing CBT For Anger Management

With Cognitive Behavioral Therapy, people can learn to tame their anger and direct such energy positively and productively. With CBT therapy, you get to:

- Know the origin of your anger as well as things that fuel it

- Learn to control and subdue emotional reactions that cause an outburst

- Communicate effectively, rather than resort to unhelpful angry emotions

- Learn how to channel your anger into enhancing your life and relationship positively.

- Learn some helpful anger management techniques to make you come off as assertive without throwing tantrums.

Cognitive Behavioral Therapy will open you up to a series of questions and CBT assignments. The aim of this is to understand the triggers and other things that fuel your anger. Once you get a grip of the anger and the root causes, you can have a range of question and techniques to experiment with. With this, you get what works best for you.

With time, you can develop effective ways of managing anger. The aim of this is the ability to confront situations objectively without the need for an unhelpful emotional outburst.

More of this will be explored in the next chapter.

Chapter 10:
Anger Management CBT Techniques That Work

I recall a client who throws a tantrum whenever her husband breaks her rigid rule of right and wrong. One day at the local grocery store, she was so enraged that she yelled at him and made a scene. When she snapped out of this state, she was embarrassed to find out that she has caused a scene and people have gathered around.

In the process of getting angry, she zoned out. This is common for many people when angry. It is like they translated to another planet entirely where they only focus on their rage and are not aware of what is going on. In the case of extreme anger, these people lose touch with reality and their senses becomes suspended which makes them unaware of the consequence of their actions.

Many people become gripped by anger before they can reason. Anger is a different emotion which grips people faster. Besides, when people get angry, they do not have the luxury of thinking which is where the problem lies. When emotions get ahold of you, your rational thinking ability will be suspended.

In exploring, our CBT can help with anger management, we need to know how anger works on us.

Exploring the Impact of Emotion

Part of the aim of having emotions is to get us moving. We have feelings that drive us away or towards the something for instance, emotions like terror, fear, and reluctance repel us from the source. While emotions like love, excitement, addiction, and anger as well bring us closer.

In therapy, it has been found that people who suffer from emotions that repel them always look forward to improvement and changes, unlike people whose emotions bring them towards something, for instance, addiction.

Anger: A Strange Seduction

Anger is in the class of emotions, like lust, which makes us focus. The bright side of anger is that it can save us since it activates the fight or flight mood. With anger, we can channel its power to stand up for ourselves.

Anger transforms us into a state where we see the world in a transparent state. We get this unexplainable certainty and courage that makes us feel stronger. However, the underlying feelings that come with anger (loss of consciousness and feeling of power) could become addictive.

Therefore, you have to be motivated and willing to get rid of anger and its hold on you. Get it in control before it starts controlling you. The following pointers will help you understand and accept why anger should be nipped.

It Is Dangerous

One of the many problems with anger is that both the enraged person and the people around suffer. Not only does it strain relationships, but it also destroys careers and might cause physical injury in some cases.

Extreme anger is dangerous and affects the normal functioning of the heart and the immune system. This is beside the physical injury it causes innocent people. Besides, the inability to suppress anger could lead to an early grave. It is so bad for the heart that inadequate exercise and smoking doesn't affect the heart as much as it does.

There is also the fact that uncontrolled anger leads to significant mistakes, mistakes that could have been averted.

Anger Makes Us Stupid

I remember a very young kid during one of my therapy sessions. His mother dragged him to therapy because of the extent of his anger. This brilliant young man almost killed his mother in the heat of anger. Well, this boy was able to control himself, but it was a problem for him and a pretty stupid thing to attempt. What if he can't restrain himself the next time he is enraged? Had he succeeded in carrying out this plan, his life would have changed forever. This is a silly thing to do but anger suspends our rational thinking capacity and we become stupid when angry.

Think about all the things you did in the heat of anger and were ashamed of when you calmed down. This, in CBT, is called emotional hijacking which is common when people get angry.

Vital Cognitive Steps to Suppress Anger

Address the Feeling First

It is easy for people to get angry before they have the chance to think. Therefore, a critical step in handling anger is to know how to get ahold of this emotional response. This must precede dealing with the thoughts that go with the feeling of excitement.

You can help yourself be alert and sensitive to anger such that you nip it before escaping and becoming uncontrollable.

You can attempt this famous 7/11 breathing technique which involves:

- Stop
- Direct your attention to your breath
- Breath in and count 7 in your mind
- Breath out slowly and count 11 inside as well

The magic happens during the breathing out process because this is when you get to relax and let go of the rage.

This might take a minute to complete but you will notice that you feel better afterward and more in control of your emotions, rather than your emotions controlling you. You can think straight and be aware of the glaring and dangerous consequence of getting angry.

Emotional Blueprint Exchange

To an angry person, the brain is configured in a way of responding to unpleasant stimuli. Hence, we can get help by learning to reconfigure the brain such that the old pattern disappears.

- You can explore how you react when you get angry. To do this, take the following step:

- Think back to a time you were outraged. All you must do is close your eyes and recall. This can happen under 10 seconds.

- Open your eyes and record how you feel. You might have a reaction to the event the same way it happened.

Part of the intention of CBT therapy for anger is for you to realize that you can transform the experience you had then such that you get to learn something about it, rather than being clouded with rage

- Next, open your eyes and try to recall the event and dissociate yourself from it. In other words, be an observer. This will reduce the emotions that come with such a memory.

- With this, you get to notice things you couldn't notice before about you and other people involved in the event. Since the emotion is calmed, your brain can objectively observe.

- Open your eyes and consider the difference in this way of accessing your memory. Many people will see this as a revelation, yet it is something that has always been there, only clouded by the rage

- Create an emotional blueprint by going back to the memory as an observer again. This time engage your creativity and observe how things would be way different if you had suppressed your rage.

- With this kind of mental rehearsal, you get to explore how things would have been different had you learned to keep your anger in check.

- After you have succeeded in calming your emotional mind and get the automatic emotional response that follows anger in check, you can proceed to employ these cognitive techniques to help with anger management.

First Technique: Create A Difference Between Your Personality and Anger

A person prone to anger will hardly admit that they need help. Besides, trying to label the person as an angry person might be a futile effort. This is because they are usually combative and ready to challenge all sort of labeling.

Hence, in helping yourself change the way you talk about it will force the brain to dissociate your personality from the anger. Therefore, consider asking yourself things like:

- How has this anger made my life worse?

- How has it caused me to misbehave?

The idea is to come to terms with the fact that you are not the anger. Hence, you can confront it. We are not trying to say you are not responsible for getting angry. But it is good to acknowledge the fact that you are willing to get help and there is a part of you that wants to do away with it. This is not surprising as people lose a lot from intense anger.

You can even consider or imagine what the anger would sound and look like. One woman told me that the anger was "like a selfish beast that will instead get her way rather than consider others' feelings".

It is not about killing the beast; I told her. We must consider what fuels the monster!

Second Technique: Identify Your Needs

Emotions are signals coming from your body. Anger is like a signal to fight and stand up for ourselves. The problem, however, lies in the fact that these signals are sometimes wrong. This is the same way a faulty car alarm can go off when there is no real threat. Have in mind that some basic emotional human needs must be continuously met healthily. If not, the consequence can be devastating.

With the above in mind, whenever you are angry, ask yourself what you want that you are not getting. A woman during one of my therapy sessions realized her husband was not always there for her. She discussed this with her husband who adjusted adequately.

She admitted that "It suddenly felt so insensitive of her to throw tantrums like a spoilt brat because her husband was busy making ends meet."

Also, sometimes getting angry seems justifiable. However, by getting to know where the gap in our needs is, we can get a break and consider how to meet such demand.

Rather than come off as threatening and authoritative, we can learn to be assertive.

The final technique helps you consider anger from the third person perspective. This will help you take charge of thoughts that trigger anger.

Third Technique: Stop Thinking Like A Dictator

Retraining Your Brain with Cognitive Behavioral Therapy

One common attribute of people with anger issues, depression, and anxiety is the pattern of thinking. Their vocabulary is full of words like 'always,' 'completely,' 'never,' 'entirely' etc.

We explored this in the third chapter that dealt with cognitive distortion. Known as black and white thinking, it is common with depressed people. All angry people approach reality with an "all or nothing" mentality. This becomes more intense, the more emotional we get. Our thought pattern reflects this as we get enraged.

Strong emotions rewire our brain to think in absolute terms, which in turn fuels our emotion. To learn how to get a grip on your anger, consider reducing this absolute thinking pattern. Asking questions that requires a less absolutist answer can help reconfigure the thinking pattern:

- Can someone take offense even if no harm was meant?

- Do people, during the heat of the anger, feel they are right? Only to calm down and consider another people's view?

- Can anger make an intelligent person do stupid things?

The ability to consider the bigger picture or view things from other people's angle is a good way to reduce the effect of anger. Do not forget that anger thrives on the rigid perception that people hold on to.

All in all, it is essential to build the desire to stay away from anger. This happens by exposing the damage that anger causes for you and others. The next step involves altering the preset emotional response to anger that we have been so used to over time.

It is also essential to dissociate anger from our personality by being careful of our choice of language which in turn influences how we process it. With this, we can seek ways to meet our needs – both physically and emotionally. And finally, we can learn to adjust our all or nothing pattern of thinking.

Chapter 11:
Be Kind to Yourself with Self-Compassion

CBT revolves around the idea that people's thought patterns, emotions, and resulting behavior are linked. Hence, any change to either of them can change the others. CBT exists in various forms, all intending to help people with multiple types of mental disorders.

The goal of CBT, in this case, is to develop a healthy coping mechanism to face life and all it throws at you. It is important to note that the journey is not going to be smooth. But with determination and discipline, you can drive yourself to the bus stop of success with CBT.

Besides, this book is about using CBT to help yourself. Hence, you are your therapist and you need to take it easy to avoid overdriving yourself. There are days you will lose motivation and the zeal to keep going. It is all part of the journey. Keep the following in mind to have an effective CBT technique at home:

Be Patient with Yourself
Oh, that change you are desperate for will not come overnight. The fact that you are trying it on your own means your patience must be more.

Instead, part of your goals should be developing your skills such that you can successfully put your mental health in check.

There will be little victories – celebrate them. With time, you will grow towards achieving your goals. There will be changes, no matter how small, be proud of them. Also, come to terms with the fact that your progress might not be linear. There will be excellent and easy weeks while others could leave you frustrated. It is all part of the journey.

Be Kind to Yourself
You can be so hard on yourself that you become so soaked in negative self-thought without realizing. However, being too hard on yourself will end up killing the zeal to work harder.

Negative thoughts will creep in and you cannot help it. However, the goal is to clip its wings before it takes root. Hence, when you have thoughts like "I suck at everything I do," or "I knew I was going to mess this up" – replace this with something pretty kind. Since it is improbable that your loved ones say things like this to you, don't think them.

This, however, is not a license to indulge yourself for wrongdoings. Instead, encourage yourself that all will be well — more on self-compassion in the next section.

Do What You Love
Mental health issues have a way of robbing you of things that matter in life. You find no joy in going to the dance, Friday night hangout means

nothing to you anymore. Hence, you will slightly curl up on your bed and play video games or watch movies. This might be due to the absence of motivation or just plain fear.

However, strive to adopt one or two things that meant something to you in the past into your schedule. We understand this is a lot to ask, but it could help your progress.

Believe in Yourself

One of the best things about CBT is the hope of a bright and better future, way better than what you have now. CBT is optimistic which teaches people that change is possible, and you can make the transition possible. Even though you do not see any shred of evidence that a change is in sight.

One common factor about anxiety, worry, depression, phobia, etc. is a false belief in which the victim holds on to something not right. Something that stops them from living life to the fullest and enjoying yourself. Since there is no evidence that the thing holding you back will happen, let go of the thought and do what you love. You will feel better.

Helping Yourself Through Self Compassion

Self-compassion for yourself is not so different from when you have it for others. In understanding this, what does self-compassion feel like? For you to be compassionate towards another person, you have got to pay attention and be aware of the person's suffering. Ignoring the beggar who asked for a dollar means you haven't taken the time to understand what he is going through.

Also, compassion involves being moved by the pains and struggles of others which push you to respond in any way to try to alleviate their suffering.

Merriam-Webster dictionary defines compassion as "a feeling of wanting to help someone sick, in trouble or hungry."

Also, compassion to others means you are kind and understanding to others when they fail or fall short of standards. This is the opposite of making harsh judgments.

Now when we talk about self-compassion, it involves practicing being kind and understanding to yourself when you fail or pass through a difficult time. Hence, you do not judge or criticize yourself when you fail. Self-compassion doesn't involve restricting yourself from getting better and doing what makes you perfect. However, it involves coming to terms with the fact that you are a human who is not perfect.

You will set goals and at times fail to meet them. Your journey to recovery might not be as smooth as you want it to be. In your goal to recovery and developing your mental health, you will make mistakes and fall short. There is no big deal in this as humans are not wired with perfections in their DNA. If you can accept this reality, developing self-compassion comes easy.

The Tripod of Self Compassion

Self-Kindness Vs. Self-Judgment

When we fail and fall short of expectations, remaining warm and understanding is what self-compassion entails. This is different from ignoring the pain or bombarding ourselves with criticism. For you to practice self-compassion, you have got to come to terms with the fact that you will be faced with difficulties and fail at times. Hence, in times like this, the ideal response of a self-compassionate person is to be gentle instead of getting all worked up when things don't go as expected.

We tend to cause ourselves unnecessary stress and frustration when we fight against these things rather than accepting it. Accepting this reality brings self-compassion.

Common Humanity Vs. Isolation

When things do not go our way, we tend to be frustrated and feel isolated. We think we are the only one making such a mistake while others have a rosy life. On the contrary, being human already licensed you to the occasional failure and imperfections.

In other words, with self-compassion comes the realization that personal inadequacy is an experience common to all humans.

Mindfulness Vs. Over-Identification

Negative emotions will inevitably arise but with self-compassion, we can take a balanced approach to it rather than try to suppress or exaggerate it. We can get this balanced view when we relate our experience with others passing through the same thing. We can also identify this when we are willing to access our negative emotions and thoughts with clarity and openness which puts them in mindful awareness. With mindfulness, you get to observe your thoughts and feelings as they arise without interfering.

Ignoring our pain cannot make us compassionate. However, mindfulness teaches that we should not get so carried away with what we are feeling that our reaction becomes negative.

How to Encourage Self Compassion Through Your CBT Journey?

"You can search throughout the entire universe for someone who is more deserving of your love and affection than you are yourself, and that person is not to be found anywhere. You, yourself, as much as anybody in the entire universe, deserve your love and affection." —Buddha

One of the most challenging parts of the journey to recovery is nurturing self-compassion. Many people can identify with this because we are the one to loudly criticize ourselves when we fall short. We are hard on ourselves to try harder and get tough.

However, in developing self-compassion you must strive to keep the love alive. Some steps to get you started on the journey to love yourself and develop self-compassion are:

See and Embrace Your Personal Goodness

Many people are laden with heavy baggage and they believe that they are wrong, which stands against self-compassion. This expresses itself when things fall apart; we had a relapse or failed to meet an expectation. In addition to the pain of what is going on, we are constantly bombarded with the thought that something is wrong with us. We embrace the belief that we are flawed, and our DNA is flawed, undeserving of love.

We, however, fail to recognize that we are pure, no matter what we think. Perfection was not built into humans, hence, give yourself a break and live your life embracing the ups and downs as they come, the success and downfall in your journey to recovery.

Accept the Validations of Others

As you strive to become the better version of yourself, there are times you will doubt your basic innate goodness. However, you can hold on to validations from others that say you are okay. You need to accept their validation and hold on to their judgment to keep you going.

When going through your CBT journey, efforts from family and loved ones can keep you going when you feel you are losing it. This class of people is essential in your recovery journey. They serve to reinforce your goodness until we come to accept and believe it.

Come to Terms with Your Imperfections

When you give up on being perfect, you will discover how amazing life is and how you have been too hard on yourself. Therefore, it is so hard for a perfectionist to try self-compassion. And besides, you have got to let go of your perfectionist attitude if you want to make considerable progress on your journey to recovery.

Think of this, it is in being perfect that you sink deep to all forms of mental health issues like addiction and depression. In contrast, however, you can learn to be vulnerable in a healthy manner. Through this, you get to develop self-love and compassion as you progress in your journey to recovery.

Lean into The Sharp Points

One trusted way to come to terms with our imperfection is to take note of the kind of thoughts and behaviors that triggers panic, anxiety, and depression. This happens when we allow ourselves to be conscious of the boundaries and expectations, we have set for ourselves.

In other words, we must embrace the path of true awakening. Keep up the hope even when you fall short. Hold on to the passion for getting better when you relapse. Get comfortable with not always meeting the target you set yourself on your journey to recovery. Do away with the panic and negative self-talk that doubt your capacity

Proven Steps to Develop Self Compassion

Your mental health might have sunk so low that you feel you are not deserving of compassion of any sort. This explains why it is hard for many people to be kind to themselves. This gets harder when we are struggling with a mental condition, yet, this is when the impact of self-compassion is most needed. We compare ourselves to sane people; get worked up at why we fail to meet expectations. We desire to be strong and criticize ourselves for failing to meet them. We conclude that we don't deserve to enjoy anything since we will likely make a fool of ourselves.

On the contrary, however, self-compassion is like the engine oil that keeps your vehicle running without friction. Self-compassion is necessary for our journey to recovery as it keeps us sane as we try to combat the ups and downs during the CBT journey.

You can develop self-compassion which will help in your journey through recovery. Some proven steps to make this happen are:

Keep Critical Comments Down

There are times you will feel so critical and aggressive towards yourself. It might be after a relapse of when you fall short of an expectation. Your progress might not be as swift as you want it which will spark disappointments and self-criticism. The key here is keeping the criticism down.

There are times you will be happy and content with yourself. Note how excited, motivated, and glad you are when you have progressed. Always cherish these moments and hope that things will get better.

Think and Speak Kindly About Yourself

In line with the first strategy, you have got to motivate yourself through your kind words. Your words are potent, and you will gradually believe what you tell yourself.

Hence, constant thinking that something is wrong with you and saying you can never get anything done right will work against your effort to get better. Bear in mind that you are different from your choices, even if you continuously make bad choices. With this, encourage yourself like you would support a friend.

Forgive Your Mistakes

Forgiveness is part of the essential strategies to develop self-compassion. No one is immune to mistakes, yet, not all take error lightly. Since you cannot go back and make amends, why not forgive yourself and move forward.

In your journey to recovery, there will be good days and bad days. You will make mistakes. The earlier you accept this as part of the recovery process, the better. Hence, avoid beating yourself up but owning up to yourself and moving on.

Keep Assumptions and Judgments Down

No one knows the future and you cannot always be right, no matter what basis, knowledge or experience with which you base your judgments and assumptions, you have. The problem with assumptions is that it limits and constricts you to a path, preventing you from exploring creativity.

People with social anxiety assume they will make a scene should they go to a party or an event. With therapy, the right care alongside self-compassion these people can develop the skills to socialize better.

Nurture Your Body and Mind

Taking care of yourself is one of the most compassionate things you can do. Fill your mind with positive thoughts. Don't deny yourself of healthy food and good company. Develop your mind with the right information and be selective regarding the company you keep.

Be attentive to learn what questions from your self-worth and others make you feel good about yourself. Armed with the awareness of what can help, strive to make compassionate choices.

It is not all about You

Many of us fail to focus on ourselves but direct all our attention to the impression that others have of us. The flaw in this is that you are most likely wrong if you think others think of you. As others might not always be thinking of you.

In developing your mental health, let go of the assumption that people are judging you and criticizing you. With time, you will understand that except for your immediate loved ones, most people do not care that you have a problem. They are only after your wellbeing which can serve as a fuel to do what is best for you.

Embracing the steps discussed above can guide you in developing self-compassion. This can determine how successful you will be with the journey to recovery.

The way you react, treat, talk, and think about yourself does not always end with you. It has a ripple effect that impacts your progress with the recovery journey as well as your relationships and choices. Hence, make self-compassion a vital component as you drive towards healing and change in your life.

Chapter 12:
Mindfulness Can Be the Difference Maker

Understanding Mindful Based Cognitive Therapy
Mindful based cognitive therapy is a form of therapy that comes from the union of cognitive therapy and meditation principles.

As a recap, we explained that CBT is a tool that helps people get ahold of their mental health by providing a solution to faulty thinking patterns.

Mindfulness, on the other hand, is the practice of paying attention to our thoughts, emotions, and feelings continually without interfering or judging them.

The combination of these two fields is a potent therapeutic tool called MBCT which has proven helpful in treating mental issues like depression, anxiety, and phobias. Mindfulness as a tool can make the process of CBT very useful. It does the following:

- With mindfulness, you get to pay attention to what you think, as well as your mood.

- With mindfulness, you get to learn how to be present and be aware of pleasures from daily living

- With mindfulness, you can stop yourself from sinking deep down the depression hole or trauma that arises from a bad mood or memories.

- With mindfulness, you can translate to a balanced and less judgmental state of mind

- You get a healthy way of dealing with unpleasant emotions and foul moods with mindfulness.

The result of combining CBT with meditation is stunning. If you believe CBT will solve your problem, try meditation as it is ten times effective. This is because CBT addresses many issues of meditation and meditation also solves many of the issues with CBT.

CBT does amplify the benefits of meditation. You calm your thoughts, relax your mind, and become more aware of the moment with meditation. There is, however, a "but" with most meditation techniques.

They do not change your thoughts. Notice in the definition of mindful meditation above, we said:

Mindfulness, on the other hand, is the practice of paying attention to our thoughts, emotions, and feelings continually without interfering or judging it.

In other words, you only get to pay attention; you neither interfere nor try to change anything. You reduce the impact the thoughts have on you. For instance, when faced with something that triggers a bad memory, mindfulness will keep you in the moment rather than making the past incident so real again which might make you zone out.

With meditation, you don't change those thoughts. Herein lies the flaw; with time, the old thoughts might creep in again if you do nothing to replace them. This is where Cognitive Behavioral Therapy comes in, as it takes care of the change process. Therefore, CBT combined with meditation is a very powerful tool.

How Does Meditation Make CBT Better?

Cognitive Behavioral Therapy helps keep tabs on negative thoughts and change them before they can affect your emotions and behavior negatively. CBT has many exercises all with a single aim – to recognize, question, and change faulty thinking patterns. We have discussed many forms of such activities in the course of this book.

Over time, these CBT exercises have been proven to work and are very useful. There is however a problem. For CBT to work and be effective with your mental issues, you need to be sensitive enough to catch those thoughts as they pop in your head.

For many people, this is not easy!

This is because some thoughts might not even last up to a second. Identifying, challenging, and changing such thoughts does not come easy. For a person using a CBT therapist, this might be easier as the job of the therapist will be to identify those faulty thought patterns through the various CBT sessions.

For someone like you conducting Cognitive Behavioral Therapy on their own, it is different. Your level of mindfulness and sensitivity needs to be high so that no thought escapes your attention. Many people are not patient enough to have this high level of awareness.

This is the impact of meditation on CBT because it makes us more aware, giving us the ability to detect and change faulty thought patterns.

A therapist might not even be able to take note of all thoughts. This is because some thoughts are so quick that there is no way they can analyze them through what you say. With meditation, however, our mind moves at our pace with a high level of awareness. This enables us to detect faulty thought patterns and change them.

A combination of meditation and CBT gives us all we need to change our thought. Besides the ability to notice and change your thoughts, there are other benefits of CBT.

Stress Reduction

Mental health issues can be exhausting. It sucks the energy out of you, removing the zeal to do anything tangible. One of the many advantages of including meditation is in stress reduction. Deep breathing, for instance, is a mindfulness practice that soothes the nervous system during stress. If the patient can learn this, they can fight the urge to react negatively in stressful situations.

An important point to note is that mindfulness gives the practitioner a greater awareness of the immediate environment and the world around them. With this, they get to appreciate life and all that happens around them, which allows for a focused priority. Besides, since mindfulness brings you to the moment, there are fewer tendencies to dwell on the future (worry and anxiety) or ruminate about the past (phobia). This practice can make the influence of CBT impactful and efficient to the patient.

Improved Mood

When mindfulness is combined with Cognitive Behavioral Practice, it is known to help improve mood – a good remedy for people dealing with depression. Not only depression but people prone to mood swings and abnormal mood responses to situations can also learn how to get ahold of their emotions via Cognitive Behavioral Therapy spiced up with meditation.

Making this a regular practice will give you a sense of purpose and connection to it. Hence, the feeling of being good for nothing, feeling lost, or worthlessness will disappear. Many have attributed this to the fact that mindfulness puts you more in tune with your environment and brings you into your daily routine making you appreciate it.

When we get involved in what we are doing rather than allowing our mind to wander around or get distracted by our thoughts, we get to appreciate things. Not only that, we get to detect our role and impact on our immediate environment and world at large. Besides, with mindfulness, the part of the brain that reduces anxiety and boosts the feeling of positivity gets activated.

Combining CBT With Meditation

The combination of these two powerful techniques will work wonder in your life. We have discussed and recommended many CBT exercises in the course of this manual. What about the meditation part?

If you do have a meditation practice in place, you will have seen its delightful effect on your CBT practice. Since Cognitive Behavioral Therapy slows down your mind, calms your nerves, and makes you more aware it will have a good impact on your CBT practice.

To get more out of your CBT when combined with meditation, we recommend the following tips:

Reduce Your Thoughts

Part of the aim of CBT is to detect thoughts, challenge them with facts, and change them. When you, however, have too many thoughts going through your mind, it gets difficult. This is because picking a thought to change becomes a challenge. Hence, we recommend reducing your thoughts. Some helpful ways to make this possible are:

Use a Mantra: this is merely a phrase that you repeat to calm your mind. This has been proven to reduce activity in the part of the brain responsible for racing and negative thoughts. Your mantra need not be something elaborate. It could be as simple as "everything will be fine," or "I will be ok." Try this several times in a day and use it to bring order to your chaotic mind.

Breathe: This brings your nervous system to the calmed state. As you breathe in, try and count to three, then to five when you exhale. Let your focus be on your breath and attempt to slow it down. Even if your mind wanders, try and bring it back.

Practice Awareness: To reduce the habit of excessive thought, form the habit of becoming aware of what is happening in the environment. When you focus on things around you, the tendency to have myriads of thoughts reduces.

Understand You cannot Predict the Future: part of the reason many have myriads of thoughts is worrying about the future. Realizing that predicting the future is not always right, no matter how much, can help limit the endless thinking you are bombarded with.

Develop Insight

For your Cognitive Behavioral Therapy endeavor to be successful, the consciousness of what is going on in your mind also matters. For many people, this could be a challenge, which is why meditation is helpful.

With meditation, our insight into what is going on in our mind increases. This awareness gives us the ability to challenge and change it. In a bid to get in tune with your thoughts, we recommend the Vipassana technique

Understanding the Vipassana Technique

Translated as light, Vipassana means a smooth awareness of all that goes on as it happens. Vipassana meditation involves the meditator using his consciousness as a tool to bring him in tune with reality. He uses his awareness to break every barrier of distraction that makes reality an illusion. It is a gradual process that involves getting in tune with how reality works.

Also known as insight meditation, it is a technique in which the meditator tunes himself to the sensation which allows one to see the true nature of existence. There are many ways of doing vipassana meditation, but a common ground for them all is the focus on breathing. The various forms of vipassana meditation employ multiple forms of focus during the process. If you want to try this vipassana meditation technique, make sure you are alone in a quiet room.

Belly as A Focus for Vipassana Technique

There are common pictures of the laughing Buddha, around which depicts Japanese tradition. This image contrasts with what many are used to (Buddha as an enlightened prince). The laughing Buddha is meant to pass Buddha off as a jovial person, especially with his large belly. The essence of the picture is not the focus, but the message hidden in the figure – the message that the stomach is essential to meditation.

The belly is seen as the center of hara, which is just below the belly button. It is the point of consciousness which many refer to as the center of the body. Directing our focus to the hara can transform us into a meditative state. On meditating with hara as the focus, your thoughts gradually reduce by themselves. Your awareness increases.

To have this form of Vipassana meditation, your attention is directed to your belly and the breathing felt around it. Breathing causes the up and down movement of the belly which is continuous. In other words, the movement of the stomach and our breath are in sync which we can use to achieve a meditative state.

Practicing the Vipassana Meditation Technique Using the Belly

Find a comfortable place and sit quietly. With your eyes closed, take in some deep breaths. Direct your focus to your stomach and watch as it moves up and down with your breath. Make sure you don't break concentration on the belly movement as it goes up and down. All your attention should be on this rhythmic movement.

With a laser focus on the belly movement, you will realize that in a couple of minutes, there will be a decrease in your thoughts as they gradually disappear. Your awareness level will soar as you feel all the processes going on in your body with this meditation process. After about 15 minutes, come out of this meditation as you take your mind away from your belly.

Make this form of meditation a daily practice. As you progress, you will discover your hara center – the center of consciousness that lies around your belly. This is the key to developing insight and awareness using vipassana meditation.

Vipassana can take many methods but we believe the above has passed the message intended. This is a very powerful ingredient that can make your CBT effort come out better.

Another Vipassana Technique: Observing Your Breath Like A River

This is another form of meditation technique based on Vipassana. It involves paying attention to the breath as it flows in and out of the body.

Just like the first method, sit down comfortably in any preferred place, free of any disturbance and distractions. Close your eyes and take in some deep breaths. After a couple of sets of breathing, start observing it. Direct all your attention on the breathing pattern and the way it goes in and out of your body. Make sure you follow the breathing with rapt attention.

The same way you go to the river on a warm afternoon. You sit down by the bank and watch as the river flows, enjoying every sensation that comes with the sight. You do not disturb yourself about the speed, direction, or manner of flow. The dirt, ripples, and quality of water do not concern you – all you do is watch.

Allow yourself to observe and pay attention to your breathing in a similar manner.

You are just a witness, and this might not be easy as there will be distractions. The thoughts will fly around. You will get distracted unawares, fight it. The key is in bringing yourself back in tune with your breath no matter how many times you get distracted. With time, your thoughts will subside, and you will get acquainted with the witness in you. This is your real and identity – the one watching the watcher.

As you proceed, keep your focus on your breathing and you get to remain in meditation.

A Ten-Minute Simple Meditation Strategy

- Get a comfortable chair and balance your feet flat on the floor. On the alternative, you can cross your legs on the floor. Whatever is convenient for you is what you should go for.

- Sit on a meditation cushion if you have one. Let it be neatly tucked under your hip bones. Your knees should fall lower than your hips

- Roll your shoulders back gently and spread your tailbone.

- Your palms might be on your knees or legs, faced up or down. Again, whatever feels natural and comfortable is what you should go for.

- Breath gently with your attention on your breath. Make it slow and note how the air fills your belly as you suck the air in and the feeling that comes with pushing the air out.

- Slowly direct your attention from your breath to the comforting sensation that comes from the coolness you feel in your nose.

- Concentrate your attention on the sensation that comes with this cool feeling.

- Gradually, you will notice how this calms your mind and all the thoughts disappear.

- For the next ten minutes, your attention should be on this coolness.

- This will translate you into a deep meditation state and with time as you make this a daily practice, you will achieve a compelling state of consciousness.

Make this meditation practice a habit as you imbibe the various CBT process we discussed in the pages of this book. You will be pleasantly surprised at how effective your CBT sessions will be with these two powerful combinations.

Conclusion

This is an indication of your zeal to get help. This excellent manual must have equipped you with an essential strategy with which you can make progress and get your mental health in order.

That you sought for help is not a sign of weakness. We have powerful and proven steps that have worked for people in the four walls of a therapist office. Hence, this manual will not leave you hanging regarding how you will help yourself.

You can get back on your feet, tame your thoughts, and shape your future. You can break free from the shackles of anxiety, depression, and thoughts holding you back. You can develop self-love and accept yourself the way you are. This love will radiate to others and transform your entire life and relationship.

You can employ the many techniques imprinted in the pages of this manual to get your life in order. You can identify the flaws in your nature, the weaknesses in your thoughts, and what is holding you back. You can take creative efforts to deal with it constructively and start radiating with a desire to conquer what life throws at you.

Retraining Your Brain with Cognitive Behavioral Therapy

You are not weak, and you are not broken. You can rise above the limitations of your thoughts and behaviors. With CBT, you can get your life back in gear, even without a therapist. Don't be distressed or overwhelmed. Even though your progress is slow, remember, it is not the first strike of an ax that cuts down the tree.

It is high time you stopped running away from your fears. It is time you stopped being a slave to your emotions and thoughts. Let this manual hold your hands, liberate you, and get you to success. Remember, fear, anxiety, phobia and all are not real. They are all in your head. But they will not leave you alone until you take the conscious effort to drive them away. You are no more the timid person controlled by fear and anxiety. Your life can make a substantial positive turn when you take the techniques presented in this manual and apply them head-on.

You can fight it, yes you can. Believe in yourself. Snap out of the thought that this is who you are. You are meant for so much more. You are not expected to live life in fear of the unknown and what is not real. You are not weak, and you are not faulty. Nothing is wrong with you. Believe in yourself and your ability to get better, believe in the various techniques imprinted in the pages of this manual. Know that you can do it even without a therapist.

As you progress in the course of this self-help therapy, celebrate your success. Approach every day with fresh hope and expectations. Know that with every day that you practice the techniques of this CBT manual, you one step closer to the person you are meant to be. The person not driven by fear or false imagination is the person whose thoughts and anxiety aren't holding them back from living life to the fullest.

You can achieve your best self again.

Celebrate your success and rejoice as you move closer to victory every day!

If you find this book helpful in anyway a review to support my endeavors is much appreciated.

www.ingramcontent.com/pod-product-compliance
Lightning Source LLC
Chambersburg PA
CBHW031116080526
44587CB00011B/999